D1613365

PROFESSIONAL
KNOWLEDGE AND SKILLS
IN THE EARLY YEARS

WITHDRAWN

LIVERPOOL JMU LIBRARY

3 1111 01 528 4480

Sara Miller McCune founded SAGE Publishing in 1965 to support the dissemination of usable knowledge and educate a global community. SAGE publishes more than 1000 journals and over 800 new books each year, spanning a wide range of subject areas. Our growing selection of library products includes archives, data, case studies and video. SAGE remains majority owned by our founder and after her lifetime will become owned by a charitable trust that secures the company's continued independence.

Los Angeles | London | New Delhi | Singapore | Washington DC | Melbourne

PROFESSIONAL KNOWLEDGE AND SKILLS IN THE EARLY YEARS

Verity Campbell-Barr

Los Angeles | London | New Delhi
Singapore | Washington DC | Melbourne

Los Angeles | London | New Delhi
Singapore | Washington DC | Melbourne

SAGE Publications Ltd
1 Oliver's Yard
55 City Road
London EC1Y 1SP

SAGE Publications Inc.
2455 Teller Road
Thousand Oaks, California 91320

SAGE Publications India Pvt Ltd
B 1/I 1 Mohan Cooperative Industrial Area
Mathura Road
New Delhi 110 044

SAGE Publications Asia-Pacific Pte Ltd
3 Church Street
#10-04 Samsung Hub
Singapore 049483

Editor: Jude Bowen
Assistant editor: Catriona McMullen
Production editor: Martin Fox
Marketing manager: Dilhara Attygalle
Cover design: Wendy Scott
Typeset by: C&M Digitals (P) Ltd, Chennai, India
Printed in the UK

© Verity Campbell-Barr 2019

First published 2019

Apart from any fair dealing for the purposes of research or
private study, or criticism or review, as permitted under the
Copyright, Designs and Patents Act, 1988, this publication
may be reproduced, stored or transmitted in any form, or
by any means, only with the prior permission in writing of
the publishers, or in the case of reprographic reproduction,
in accordance with the terms of licences issued by
the Copyright Licensing Agency. Enquiries concerning
reproduction outside those terms should be sent
to the publishers.

Library of Congress Control Number: 2018957851

British Library Cataloguing in Publication data

A catalogue record for this book is available from
the British Library

ISBN 978-1-5264-4121-8
ISBN 978-1-5264-4122-5 (pbk)

At SAGE we take sustainability seriously. Most of our products are printed in the UK using responsibly sourced
papers and boards. When we print overseas we ensure sustainable papers are used as measured by the PREPS
grading system. We undertake an annual audit to monitor our sustainability.

Thank you to my boys

Daddy, Mummy (Verity) and Reuben – drawn by Reuben, aged 9

CONTENTS

ABOUT THE AUTHOR

Verity Campbell-Barr is an Associate Professor in Early Childhood Studies at the University of Plymouth. Verity has over 15 years of experience researching the provision of early childhood services and policy developments in early childhood education and care. Her research interests centre on the quality of early childhood services, with a particular focus on the role of the early childhood workforce in supporting the quality of services. In 2015 she spent 18 months in Hungary undertaking a Marie Curie European Research Fellowship (funded by the European Commission) considering the knowledge, skills and attitudes for working in the early childhood education and care workforce. Most recently she has embarked on a research project considering interpretations of child-centred practice in different European countries in support of quality early childhood education and care. Verity can be found at @DrVerityCB.

ACKNOWLEDGEMENTS

The author and the publisher are grateful for permission to reproduce the following material in this book:

Figure 1.1 from Moloney (2010) Figure 3 in 'Professional identity in early childhood care and education: perspectives of pre-school and infant teachers', *Irish Educational Studies*, 29(2), p. 177, copyright © Educational Studies Association of Ireland, reprinted by permission of Taylor & Francis Ltd, www.tandfonline.com on behalf of Educational Studies Association of Ireland.

Figure 7.1 adapted by permission from Springer Nature: Springer, Table 1.1, Dalli, C., Miller, L. and Urban, M. (2012) 'Early childhood grows up: towards a critical ecology of the profession', in L. Miller, C. Dalli and M. Urban (eds), *Early Childhood Grows Up: Towards a Critical Ecology of the Profession*.

INTRODUCTION

My interest in professional knowledge and skills in the early years stems from two core areas. The first is in relation to debates on quality early years services and how, irrespective of the theoretical or methodological approach to explorations of quality, those who work in early years services are continually demonstrated as central to the quality of provision. Whilst I recognise that there are continued debates as to what quality is, how/if it can be assessed, its consequences for understandings of child development and its implications for early years practice (see Chapter 2), for me the centrality of the workforce for the quality of early years services raises a clear question as to what a quality workforce in the early years is. Frequently, a quality workforce is concurrent with a high level qualification (typically a university degree) and (often poorly articulated) associations with professionalism. However, the focus on qualification levels and professionalism within explorations of quality prompts a question that is my second area of interest: what should an early years qualification look like to support individuals in becoming early years professionals?

My interest in the role of a qualification to support someone in becoming a quality professional has resulted in an exploration of the knowledge and skills that are identified as being important for early years professionalism and what is my role, as a tutor involved in the delivery of degrees, in facilitating the process of an individual becoming an early years professional. As I discuss in Chapter 1, explorations of knowledge and skills and what early years qualifications might look like will be situated within a context. The context encompasses many areas, but includes considering what constitutes a profession, the role of the profession and who it is that determines this. If it is accepted that I (or any other tutor) can teach someone to be a quality professional, what should I teach, how should I teach and, importantly, what is it that I am hoping the end outcome will be at the end of teaching process? As such, the definition of a quality early years professional will ripple backwards in shaping the knowledge and skills needed to become a quality early years professional.

Determining what a quality early years professional is will be tied to constructions of the role of early years professionals that have evolved over time, encompassing subtle (and not so subtle) variations depending on the context in which the professional is working. Contextual features such as the type of service a person is working in; what is the role of the service – both in relation to policy ideals and those of the professionals working in them; the country the person is working in; the community the person is working in (e.g. urban or rural, affluent or deprived); and the children and families who are accessing the services will all shape understandings of what is a quality early years professional. Whilst it appears that my interest in exploring professional knowledge and skills in the early years has been a series of questions upon questions, I am an advocate of bringing knowledge back into the early years, seeking to explore answers to the questions rather than invoking a sense of not knowing.

Questioning is an important part of professionalism, providing the opportunity to develop a deeper understanding of one's professional role, whilst also offering opportunities to develop professional practice. Often the questioning is encompassed in the long tradition of reflective practice that is present in the early years, but I am also conscious that questioning can become an almost destructive process whereby the constant questions can result in a sense of not knowing. Therefore, central to my interest in professional knowledge and skills in the early years, is a consideration of knowledge and recognising the rich and varied ways that early years professionals know how to work with young children.

An Initial Framework

My early explorations into professional knowledge and skills in the early years focused on the European Lifelong Learning statement on competences. The European Commission identifies Key Competences for Lifelong Learning (LLL) as 'a combination of knowledge, skills and attitudes appropriate to the context' (European Commission, 2007: 3). I explore lifelong learning in more depth in Chapter 2, but here I want to consider the notion of a combination of knowledge, skills and attitudes appropriate to the context. Again the context is framed as determining what are the professional knowledge, skills and attitudes needed to meet the demands of working in the early years. The same contextual features that I outlined earlier will impact on the identification of the 'appropriate' knowledge, skills and attitudes and, whilst throughout the book I explore different contextual features, the trio of knowledge, skills and attitudes has provided me with an initial framework with which to begin to explore early years professionalism and what early years professional training might constitute.

In particular, the word attitudes has been something that I have explored in my own research. I am curious not only as to what is meant by an 'attitude' and its relationship to knowledge and skills, but also as to whether or not, as a tutor, I can teach someone the attitudes needed to support them in their pursuit of professionalism. The notion of teaching attitudes quickly proffers an appreciation that teaching is not necessarily a didactic approach, whereby students are empty vessels that I (as the 'teacher') fill with the appropriate attitudes. Rather, there are implied connotations of fostering and scaffolding appropriate attitudes.

My interest in the notion of attitudes has prompted a deeper exploration of the knowledge, skills and attitudes triad for early years professionals. The focus on the early years I think is important, as I identify those who work in the early years as being distinct in their approach to working with children. My interpretation of early years has always been one that reflects the degree that I teach on, whereby there is a focus on children (and their families) from birth to the age of eight. Embedded within this is a focus on services prior to statutory school age, reflecting a belief that there is something distinct about the early years from that of schooling; albeit a distinctness that I think schooling could gain a lot from.

As I explore in Chapter 6, the term attitudes is loosely defined and has come to be used interchangeably with beliefs, dispositions and an ethic of care, but I think that each of these terms are symbolic of the uniqueness of the early years. Embedded within this loose definition is a variable array of terms, such as love, patience and empathy, that illustrate something beyond just knowledge and skills that is important for working in the early years. As I explore in Chapter 3, what is considered knowledge is often based upon epistemological hierarchies, whereby scientific reason is regarded as the basis of knowledge. Knowledge is often equated to theory and becomes centred upon that which is written about, tested and distributed in some way. However, throughout the book I refer to knowledge**s** to reflect that I think that there are different ways in which early years professionals know how to work with children. Within my emphasis on knowledges (knowledge in the plural), I would encompass attitudes as a form of knowledge and, as I explore in Chapter 3, it is just that attitudes have different structures and processes of sharing and testing than those of theory, but are nonetheless important for early years professionals.

My focus on knowledges is about recognising the complexities of coming to know how to work with young children. As I discuss in Chapter 4, the early years draws upon a rich and varied array of disciplines that sit along the more attitudinal aspects of the profession. Choosing to be an early years professional is like choosing to study for several different degrees at once, as early years is recognised internationally as being multidisciplinary, drawing upon psychology, sociology, biology, social policy and more. In addition there are the challenges of learning to be patient and empathetic, and then on top of that you need to know about children's interests, such as dinosaurs, deep sea creatures, wild flowers, insects, fairies, cars … – the list could go on. Appreciating the intricacies of professional knowledge and skills in the early years is therefore about celebrating just how much early years professionals know, and being able to challenge any suggestion that working with children is 'easy'.

To add an additional layer to the complexities of working with young children, it is important to recognise that knowledge alone is not enough. For example, I can know how to ride a bike – the theory if you like of putting one foot on each pedal and push-ing down to generate momentum. However, the theory alone is not enough as I need to be able to put it into practice and if you consider your own experiences of learning to ride a bike, the theory is not very easy in practice. I remember watching my older brother ride his bike and thinking, 'I know what I need to do' – my grazed knees told a different story.

I am not seeking sympathy for my grazed knees, but to illustrate that knowledge has to be applied, particularly within professional contexts. The application of knowledge requires skill, but as I will discuss in Chapters 3 and 4, it is not just the skill of applying the knowledge, but in combining the different knowledges and applying them in differ-ent ways and to different extents to meet the needs of the context. Working with young children is complex, multifaceted, but also very rewarding.

The Current Climate

Throughout the book I draw upon international examples of research and practice to develop the points I am making. Whilst I would always caution against uncritically adopting the early years practice of another country and applying it in an unfamiliar context, our current early years climate is one where there is an international interest in early years services and an international sharing of ideas. The early years has a long tra-dition of sharing ideas internationally and there are many advantages to sharing ideas as they can offer different perspectives and new learning opportunities. However, different practices and approaches within the early years develop within their particular contexts, with their unique histories of early years services, and associated constructions of early years professionals, making the transposing of ideas and practice between cultural con-texts highly questionable (Oberhuemer, 2014). Further, there are stark warnings that comparative approaches should not be preoccupied with regulative performance and adherence to a common norm of early years services, but appreciative of the differences and learning opportunities they promote (Moss et al., 2016). Therefore, there is a need to read the international examples as insights into different national approaches to early years professionalism; insights that help to illustrate a point or to promote thinking and knowledge development.

Early years is international, demonstrated by the international interest in the role of early years services in supporting social welfare strategies and providing the foundations to children's lifelong learning (see Chapters 1 and 2). The international interest in early years services reflects my own developing interest in professional knowledge and skills in the early years, whereby there is an interest in quality early years services to support the wider social welfare objectives of supporting parental employment and lessening the educational inequalities between children from different socio-economic circum-stances. The international focus on quality early years services therefore encompasses an increasing international awareness and analysis of early years professionals in pursuit of quality services. Whilst there is much to be gained from this international scrutiny, it also brings challenges.

Throughout the book there are common stories surrounding early years professionals. There are stories of how early years services have developed and the distinction and combination of education and care within them, stories of the gendering of who is an early years professional and many stories of the challenges and struggles of being an early years professional. Despite the international focus on the importance of early years services in support of wider social welfare objectives, early years services predominantly remain underfunded, with poor pay and status for the professionals working within them.

Early years professionals are caught in a paradox of the international recognition of the important role that early years services have for children and their families, with increasing expectations as to what early years services can 'do' and 'achieve' and frequently inadequate rates of funding. I am often alarmed by the increasing expectations of early years professionals as being the answer to everything, whereby the 'answers' are often focused on narrow prescriptive outcomes that can measure and assess the effectiveness of early years services. Therefore, my focus on knowledges and skills is not only about appreciating and celebrating the complexities of coming to know how to work with children, but also about finding ways to recognise that knowledge is power. As knowledgeable professionals, knowledge becomes a powerful tool in resisting, working alongside or working with the ideals held by others as to what it is that an early years professional 'should' be and what it is that they 'should' do. The 'others' are not just policy makers who set the increasing expectations, as early years professionals have to negotiate the expectations of families, communities and, importantly, the children that they work with.

Being an early years professional is both challenging and rewarding, so my approach to the book has been one of setting the context, exploring what knowledge and skills are, bringing knowledge back in and recognising the rich and varied ways in which early years professionals know how to work with young children.

The Book

Chapter 1 begins with setting the context for an exploration of professional knowledge and skills in the early years. As such, the chapter briefly traces the historical development of early years services and analyses understandings of their role. This brief history leads into considering more recent developments around early years services and the international interest in the social welfare function of services that I have raised above. Against this historical backdrop I explore the gendered nature of early years services, touching on the construction of services as supporting mothers, whilst developing a gendered, mother ideal, of who is most appropriate to work with young children. I challenge this gendered ideal, cautioning against binary constructions of gender and other aspects of early years services, such as care and education. The exploration of early years services provides the context against which to consider what it means to be a professional.

In Chapter 2, I pick up on the recent historical development of early years services to analyse in more detail the story of quality and high returns and its consequences for early years professionals. In particular, I consider how the emphasis on quality has resulted in a focus on the ways in which quality can be achieved. Irrespective of the theoretical or methodological approach to the question of quality, the workforce is always identified as central, and yet, in analysing workforce requirements internationally it is possible to see a myriad of approaches to how best to train those who work with young children. I explore some of the different training models that exist and how, predominantly, they look to encompass a combination of theory and practice in providing the foundations to being an early years professional.

The combination of theory and practice begins to illustrate the different ways in which individuals come to know how to work with young children, which forms the basis of Chapter 3. In that chapter I consider what knowledge is, drawing on sociological perspectives to provide a model for considering knowledges; from theoretical knowledge to everyday knowledge (Bernstein, 1999). The focus on the everyday reflects that early years is an applied profession – knowledge alone is not enough. Early years professionals need to know not only how to apply knowledge, but also how to combine different forms of knowledge and how to evaluate the knowledge. In Chapter 4 I then explore the range of knowledges and skills for working with young children, analysing the multi-disciplinary knowledge-base of early years professionalism. I explore the relationship between know-that and know-how to analyse in a more applied way how knowledges relate to skills.

Having considered the early years professional knowledge-base, Chapter 5 supports readers to analyse their own knowledge about what childhood is and how this shapes them as early years professionals. I begin the chapter with an exploration of world views of childhood: common ways in which childhood has come to be understood. I also ask readers to consider their own world view and to analyse where it has come from, both in regard to historical constructions of childhood and their own experiences of childhood. I then question the notion of a global childhood, particularly in relation to the international interest in early years services and whether this is resulting in a convergence of ideas on childhood. My conclusion is that whilst there are commonalities, it is important to recognise the multiplicities of childhoods that exist internationally, nationally and even within individual communities.

In Chapter 6, I establish that the origins of the profession are grounded in a socially expected morality. As a part of the moral expectations of professions, individuals learn appropriate emotional responses that are an expected part of the cultural context as well as expected of the profession. Using the shorthand of emotionology, I consider how emotions are focused on the other and recognise the ways in which early years professionals engross themselves in the other – the other being the child. I discuss that there are multiple ways to refer to emotionology and even more ways in which to describe it, suggesting that the early years professional community is only at the start of articulating, distributing and validating this form of knowledge.

Chapter 7 focuses on the place of experiences for providing an empirical theory of how the world is. Through everyday observations and interactions individuals learn about the communities that they are in. Through training to work with young children, early years professionals develop an additional layer to their empirical theory as to how to interact and how to be with children. The experiences of working with children provide an important part of the early years professional knowledge-base, but experience alone is not enough to be an early years professional. Experience alone risks de-intellectualising professional practice, individualising expertise and assuming that a professional is at their pinnacle on the day that they retire. Thus, whilst reflective practice is a useful tool for learning from experiences, it needs to encompass both theory and practice. I therefore return to the work of Bernstein (1999) to consider the coming together of theory and practice, before utilising Bronfenbrenner's (1979) ecological model as a visual representation for considering the different layers that shape professional practice.

In the Conclusion I acknowledge that the book is not an exhaustive analysis of knowledges and skills for the early years, as there are areas such as Children's Rights and Special Educational Needs that I only briefly touch upon, but are nonetheless important for early years professionalism. However, in acknowledging that the book cannot include a full and detailed analysis of *all* knowledges and skills, I conclude by focusing upon the rich and varied ways that early years professionals know how to work with young children. My hope is that in reading the book, early years professionals will recognise, appreciate and celebrate just how knowledgeable and skilled they are.

1

WHAT DOES IT MEAN TO BE A PROFESSIONAL IN THE EARLY YEARS?

Early years services and those who work in them are shaped by a range of different histori-cal, social and economic factors that have consequences for answering the question *what does it mean to be a professional in the early years?* In this chapter I trace the historical develop-ment of early years services, including the influence of gender norms, economics and social policy in different international contexts to contemplate their consequences for interpret-ing what is meant by the terms 'early years' and 'professional'. I consider interpretations of early years services as care, education or educare and how this impacts on understandings of professional roles. I explore how early years professionals often become the sites at which different ideas on early years services converge. In recognising that being an early years professional positions one as being the meeting point for different perspectives on early years services, it is possible to analyse how interpretations of 'professional' have developed. In exploring what it means to be 'professional' readers are encouraged to consider their own perspective and develop their own interpretations to meet their own contexts.

Socio-cultural Histories and Early Years Services

History provides an understanding of how people saw things at other times (Parker-Rees, 2015), eliciting interpretations for the present. Looking at history offers an understanding of how early years services came to be provided and what has informed the structuring of services and those who work in them. History presents particular narratives on early years services (Selbie and Clough, 2005) – common stories that shape the social meanings of what it means to be an early years professional.

Historically children were seen as small adults (McGillivray, 2008), but as concepts of childhood changed (see Chapter 5), so did understandings of children's needs and the services that they required. The invention of childhood established the idea that children are different from adults and therefore require different experiences and services (see Gabriel, 2017). In the 1700s, there was the start of education for young children; driven by social, political and religious motivations (Nutbrown and Clough, 2014). A romantic, child saving discourse, stimulated by a desire to protect children from the harsh realities of the industrial world (Gabriel, 2017), was pivotal in establishing children as distinct to adults. The exact period of **Romanticism** is disputed, so the term is used here to represent a philosophical thinking that is frequently attributed to the work of Rousseau and the natural child, predisposed to learning (Campbell-Barr, 2014). The romantic concept is one whereby educators draw on the natural potential within a child, often through sensory explorations, rather than didactic approaches to learning, and can be attributed as being the origins of early years services.

In the 1800s the romantic education movement became more established, concerned with developing education around the needs of the child, fuelled by growing social concerns about child poverty (Nutbrown and Clough, 2014). Early years pioneers such as Pestalozzi, Froebel, the McMillan sisters and Isaacs can all be (albeit not exclusively) identified as a part of this Romantic Movement (Aslanian, 2015; Nutbrown and Clough, 2014). For example, the McMillan sisters' Open Air Nursery School (established in London in 1917) can be seen as a romantic response to the needs of children, whereby children (and childhood) were lost and needed rescuing (McGillivray, 2008).

Early years pioneers were not the only ones influenced by the Romantic Movement. Novelists such as Charles Dickens and artists such as William Blake also contributed to a wider Romantic Movement, as did theorists who have contributed to understandings of child development. For example, developmental psychology supported the distinction between childhood and adulthood, identifying a process whereby children go from immaturity to maturity (Gabriel, 2017).

> By the early 20th century, Freud had developed the romantic internalisation
> of childhood in his model of the childish id, the adult ego, and the parental/social
> super-ego but children had already effectively been removed from most areas of adult life.
> (Parker-Rees, 2015: 199)

This romantic conception of children is important in shaping the way in which early years services developed a view of services in a custodial sense, where the well-being of the child is nurtured and protected (Jensen et al., 2010). Such views of children and their learning have a lasting legacy in the UK and beyond and are evident in understandings of early years practice today (Pound, 2011; Selbie and Clough, 2005), whereby those who work in early years services still identify with the desire to nurture and protect children (McGillivray, 2008).

The Romantic Movement has a lasting legacy in understandings of early years services internationally, but this did not translate into widespread early years services. For example, in the UK, early years services were targeted at children identified as being the most in need (Randall, 2000), with levels of provision ultimately remaining low in comparison to the child population. Increases in early years provision did occur during both the First and Second World War to support female employment as part of the wider war efforts, shifting services away from being only to support the children most in need. However, such initiatives did not translate into a lasting legacy of widespread early years provision as the traditional male breadwinner model was reaffirmed after the wars. The model reflected a desire to dissuade women from working to ensure there was employment for the men returning from war, as well as a response to the negative consequences of child evacuation (Randall, 2000). In particular, child evacuation had raised questions of children's lack of attachments to a primary carer and the negative consequences for a child's healthy development. Early years services therefore returned to a concept of meeting the needs of children in extreme circumstances.

Beyond the UK, other countries had their own evolution of early years services. In Hungary, historically important moments, alongside its socio-political history, have shaped the character of early years provision. For example, whilst Hungarian early years services have been influenced by Pestalozzi and Rousseau (Nagy Varga et al., 2015), there has also been a strong folk culture that has seen the incorporation of folk music, dance and art into early years services. Following the Second World War, the influence of Soviet politics meant that kindergartens were nationalised and expected to follow a centralised, Soviet, model. Early years services were recognised for their role in educating 'socialist citizens' whilst also supporting women's mass employment (Nagy Varga et al., 2015). The fall of **Communism** has seen a resurgence of Hungarian folk traditions within early years services as part of a more Hungarian (nationalistic) education model.

Early years services are, therefore, cultural sites (Tobin, 2005) that represent a meeting of social values on the care and education of young children, combined with views on the family. Social values will have developed over time and demonstrate a historical evolution in the ways in which different cultural contexts shape understandings about children, care, education and family life. Whilst there are commonalities in the historical evolution of early years services in different international contexts, it is important to recognise that countries are at different points on a historical journey in developing early years services. The history that I present is largely influenced by my British heritage, but there will be elements of it that are familiar in other international contexts. However, historically important moments will affect social values and can act as an impetus for a change of direction in the ways of thinking about early years services in different international contexts. Exploring both historical and international examples of early years services therefore helps to elicit an appreciation of the taken-for-granted and different cultural interpretations.

Early years services have a long history of sharing ideas on the care and education of children. However, the sharing of ideas on early years services has never been greater, facilitated by the internet, alongside **supra-national organisations** such as the World Bank, OECD and Unicef advocating investments into early years services, whilst also undertaking international reviews of early years services (Campbell-Barr and Leeson, 2016; Miller and Cameron, 2014). The international sharing of structural and interpretative features of early years services is arguably creating a convergence of ideas in the ways of thinking about early years services and those who work in them. Supra-national organisations, which do not have the power to dictate national policy, but nonetheless seek to influence its direction, increasingly offer advice and guidance on the provision of early years services (Campbell-Barr and Bogatić, 2017). For example, the United Nations' Sustainable Development Goals (United Nations, 2015) state that:

> By 2030, ensure that all girls and boys have access to quality early childhood development, care and preprimary education so that they are ready for primary education.

The goal illustrates that countries are at different stages of developing their early years services (along a spectrum of no services, to fully funded access for all children). The goal also presents a particular story of early years services, whereby quality services are important for children's education and for ensuring equality of access to the educational advantages of early years services (see Chapter 2 for further discussion). However, the common goal for quality services to support children's development will meet with other stories about the provision of early years services (such as the romantic interventionist story), which reflect different socio-cultural contexts. These different stories explain why, despite common global goals for early years services, the implementation varies in different contexts. Those working in early years services can find themselves negotiating the varying stories that exist about early years services as the development of new stories does not mean old ones go away (Campbell-Barr and Bogatić, 2017).

A Recent History of Early Years Services

The historical evolution of early years services demonstrates how there are two core strands around understanding their role. One strand relates to the romantic discourse, whereby early years services are to support and nurture children, particularly those identified as being the most in need. The second strand is the role of early years services in supporting maternal employment. Inevitably, different countries have engaged with these two strands in variable ways at different points in history, but the dual elements have provided a lasting legacy in the conceptualisation of early years services that is present today. However, international examples illustrate how levels of early years provision are not just the product of conceptualisations, but subject to a willingness to invest in, and political commitment to, services. Thus, whilst some countries have witnessed political support for early years services, facilitated by financial investments, other countries have seen the emergence of mixed market models, dominated by private, voluntary and independent (PVI) enterprises (of varying scales), seeking to provide a service when the state government is not.

The UK offers an example of where a historical lack of political interest in early years services resulted in a reliance on a mixed market model (Penn, 2012a). Changing family structures and social expectations meant that increasing numbers of women entered employment, with the market responding by providing early years services. As such, early years businesses of varying scales and types (e.g. day nurseries, childminders, pre-schools) began to emerge to provide services for families. However, the reliance on the market meant that levels of provision were inconsistent across the country. Therefore, when the Conservative government of the 1990s began to offer some level of financial support for early years services the schemes were hampered by insufficient levels of provision (Randall, 2000).

In 1997, the New Labour government was elected and early years services became a policy priority. The 1998 National Childcare Strategy was something of an early years landmark in the UK, signalling a political interest in the accessibility, affordability and quality of early years services. Since 1998, early years services have witnessed a policy explosion, with continued developments to address the quality, affordability and accessibility of services. However, whilst levels of early years provision have expanded since 1998, there remain questions as to the core social policy function of early years services; whether affordability for parents is at the expense of those providing early years services, as well as much discussion as to the meaning of quality (Campbell-Barr, 2015; Moss, 2014a). I return to the question of quality in the next chapter as it is central to debates on early years services, but important to note here is that early years professionals have become policy objects – objects that are expected to deliver policy intentions and are shaped by those intentions.

Whilst the National Childcare Strategy marks an important turning point in the development of early years services, there have been mixed political messages as to what is the role of services. Since 1998, the policy rationale for investing in early years services has represented two equality drivers: one to ensure all parents can access employment and the second, to ensure children have access to the educational advantages of early years services (Campbell-Barr, 2015; Moss, 2014a). Meeting these dual objectives has often proved challenging. One key challenge is that affordability, which has been a central theme within early years policy in the UK, has focused on the needs of parents. For example, the issue of affordability saw the introduction of both free early years services for three and four year olds (and, later, some two year olds), whilst also offering tax incentives for working parents accessing childcare for children of all ages. The varying funding schemes demonstrate that affordability was (and is) about parents, whereby services are free at the point of use or subsidised in relation to the parents' circumstances.

I do not question the importance of ensuring that early years services are affordable, but the focus on parents creates questions as to the position of those providing early years services. There are continued messages about the challenges early years providers face regarding underfunding (West and Noden, 2016) and poor pay (Georgeson and Payler, 2014; Moss, 2006). Affordability for parents is therefore not matched with sustainability for early years providers.

Embedded in both the history and recent policy developments of early years services are a number of stories that entwine around the dual strands of supporting children's needs and facilitating maternal employment. Within these dual strands, there are two stories that I think have a lasting legacy for shaping understandings of what is an early years professional. One story is that of gender and **feminism**, whereby the positioning of early years services as supporting equality of access to the labour market for mothers combines with a historical legacy of women being responsible for meeting the needs and supporting the rights of children. The second, related story is that of the relationship between care and education in understanding the role of early years services. I will consider both of these stories in turn, before going on to consider a third story, that of the increasing expectations of early years professionals.

Gender and Feminism

The historical evolution of early years services is undoubtedly bounded by debates on gender. The consequences of these debates are complex and multifaceted, represented by discussions on the gendered nature of the workforce, the position of the maternal discourse in understanding the supply and demand of early years services and what it means to be an early years professional. The debates on gender have their origins in the history of early years services and the **philanthropic** and romantic drivers present in the early stages of establishing early years services. Press (2015) provides a comprehensive overview of the history of early years professionalism that took place in Australia, which resonates with the histories of other countries, whereby the development of early years services has a history of the dual strands of supporting children and women. The positioning of early years services as supporting maternal employment demonstrates a clear gendering, but the philanthropic and romantic origins of early years services also provided gendered messages as to who was best placed to support children.

Press (2015) outlines the developments of the early years workforce in Australia and how philanthropic and romantic drivers perpetuated a maternal discourse that both devalued the work of early years professionals, and potentially demonised 'bad' mothers. The romantic motivation to want to nurture and protect (vulnerable) children required individuals – women – to fulfil the nurturing role. Lazzari (2012) explores the maternal discourse in early years services in Italy, arguing that this has resulted in a construction of women having a natural disposition to work with young children. In Italy there is a romantic history to early years services, whereby the nurturing of children is regarded as a gendered activity (Caruso and Sorzio, 2015). The natural associations within the romantic discourse pertain to a **hetero-normativity** that has positioned women as natural carers (Andrew et al., 2016). However, the combination of the romantic and philanthropic motivations meant that the nurturing was done as a contribution to society, not as paid employment. Further, the naturalness positioned the looking after of young children as not requiring any particular knowledge or skills. The consequences of the romantic and philanthropic history of early years services are that of a low status and low paid profession to be undertaken by women.

The hetero-normativity of women as natural carers constructs the knowledge and skills required for working in the early years as somehow innate. The innate construct devalues working in early years services as it is something that women are seen as 'naturally' able to do. As an advocate of early years professionals being knowledgeable and skilled, the innate construct is a view that I challenge throughout this book. I do not think it is possible to determine that a person is born able to work with young children on the basis of their gender. My concerns with the innate construct are that it excludes men from being able to 'do' caring, devalues the challenges of learning how to work with young children and labels women who are not able to 'do' caring as somehow unnatural. In particular, I find the hetero-normative position of women as natural carers and men as not particularly problematic as it not only excludes men from the early years, thus potentially reducing the labour force by half, it also limits the potential of having a diverse workforce with a variety of knowledges and skills. My fear is that the gendered nature of who is an early years professional is so deeply engrained in hetero-normative, innate and gendered attributes for describing early years professionals (Jones, 2015) that it might not be possible to move beyond them (Cameron, 2001, 2006).

Post-structural perspectives have challenged biological determinism (Osgood and Robinson, 2017) and have already undertaken to contest the innate construct. Post-structural perspectives question the certainty of scientific (biological) knowledge, challenging that there is absolute knowledge (Campbell-Barr and Leeson, 2016; Osgood and Robinson, 2017), such as one way in which to be a man or woman. In challenging that there is one rational and coherent form of knowledge, post-structural perspectives identify with the complexities of human existence whereby there is more than one possibility – more than one story of how to be a man or woman.

Post-structural accounts have sought to more than contest hetero-normativity, by also exploring how dominant discourses seek to discipline human behaviour. Discourses represent dominant ways of thinking, viewing and speaking about a particular subject – the dominant, taken-for-granted stories. Discourses normalise behaviour to the extent that the biases and assumptions that have informed them are invisible. Discursive constructions of gender have therefore created stories as to what it means to be a man or a women, whilst masking the who, what and why of the forming of the stories. Historical accounts of women's experiences and position within society illustrate that the moral standards of women came to signify the success of a society (Skeggs, 1997). Considering women who care for young children became all the more important as women are tasked with the responsibility of civilising the next generation. Those entering early years services therefore do so with a long history of classifying moral behaviours. Women are given constant messages about right and wrong behaviours that are closely aligned to cultural discourses on femininity and motherhood. Thus who is an early years professional is not just about gender, but also about a particular performance of gender.

Post-structural approaches have been applied to more than just the question of who is an early years professional. As will be raised in the next chapter, they have been used to develop a critique of both child development and concepts of quality. Whilst post-structural approaches open up the possibility of telling more than one story about early years professionalism, child development or quality, those working in early years services become a meeting point for the different theoretical perspectives. The result is that biologically deterministic and post-structural views coexist. Thus, whilst there are many examples of literature that seek to challenge understandings of early years professionalism and the position of gender within this (Andrew et al., 2016; MacNaughton, 1997, 2005; Osgood, 2006, 2009; Vandenbroeck and Peeters, 2008), for those working in early years services they may not necessarily relate to these critical perspectives of gender and professionalism. There are those who chose to become an early years professional as they identify it as a feminine occupation. Research has shown that women chose to work with young children as they see it as a profession that they can 'do', drawing on the innate construct (Miller, 2008; Penn, 2011; Skeggs, 1997; Vincent and Braun, 2011). Being an early years professional is therefore about negotiating the different theoretical perspectives – being the meeting point for different stories of early years services.

I am conscious that the story of gender in relation to who is an early years professional is closely related to stories on motherhood and I have touched on some of these above. Whilst the hetero-normativity has positioned women as natural carers, it has also raised questions as to the position of mothers within society. The provision of early years services to support maternal employment reflects equality drivers whereby all women should have equality of access to the labour market. However, views on women working have shifted over time, illustrated by the post Second World War period, where women went from the public sphere of working to support the war effort to returning to the private sphere of home. Views on women and employment therefore represent another example of new and old ideas coming together, whereby the notion of a 'good' mother can be both a working mother and one who stays at home. Debates on motherhood are beyond my focus, but have been considered by others (Duncan and Edwards, 1997; Hakim, 2000; Thomson et al., 2011). What readers should be aware of is how different stories do not occur in isolation and will have consequences for each other.

Education, Care or Educare

The socio-historical evolution of early years services demonstrates the variations and commonalities that exist in how early years services have been conceptualised. The role of early years services as education, care or educare has already been touched upon, but now I want to focus on considering whether early years services are there to provide care for children, to educate children or to do a combination of these. The brief overview of the historical developments of early years services has demonstrated how early years services reflect socio-cultural understandings on how to best care for and educate children. What has emerged and changed with time is a structuring of early years services as being either care, education or educare focused as a result of the age of the child and different interpretations of services. The focus of early years services is important as it has consequences for who is an early years professional in regard to whether they are education, care or educare professionals. Therefore, in this section, I look at the structure of early years services in order to lead into a discussion of understandings of professional roles and professionalism.

There is a historical divide between childcare and early education services that has its origins in the development of formal, centre-based, early childhood services in the 19th century (Moss, 2006). The division of services created a demarcation in conceptualising the role and purpose of services and those who work in them. Divisions between early years services are not just conceptual and structural, but are also deeply embedded in how the public think about services (Moss, 2006). Often referred to as split models, many countries divide early years services between those for children from birth to three years of age and those for children from three to school age. Services for younger children (birth to three) are identified as 'care' based, offering replacement care whilst parents access the labour market. Such services include childcare centres, nurseries and crèches. Services for older children (three to school age) are identified as early education, represented by nursery schools, preschools, *écoles maternelles* and nursery classes. Often care and education services fall under the political responsibility of different government departments. The division creates a persistent divide between types of early years services, those who work in them, children's development and conceptualisations of care and education (Oberhuemer, 2005). At the most simplistic level, there is an underlying assumption that younger children are not being educated, but only cared for, and that older children somehow lose their care needs on their transition to an education-based service. Emphasising the transition not only illustrates an artificial divide between care and education, it also highlights how a split model can create multiple transitions for children, at a time when security and consistency are key to their development.

Given the concerns with the split model, both conceptually and practically, supra-national organisations such as the OECD and European Commission advocate a more integrated model. The integrated model treats the birth to school age as a holistic developmental stage, requiring a blend of education and care focused services, with all services being the responsibility of one government department. The integrated model is well illustrated by the Nordic countries, such as Denmark, Sweden and Finland, that have a history of adopting the integrated model since the 1970s. For these countries, the integrated model is about more than just integrating the provision of care and education services. For example, Finland's early years policy adopts an integrated model as a part of a comprehensive welfare offer that provides early years services alongside a range of other family-friendly policies, such as maternity and paternity leave, and represents an active political decision to develop and invest in early years services (Lundkvist et al., 2017; Nygård and Krüger, 2012). Whilst austere times have resulted in a review of public spending on family welfare initiatives in Finland, the integrated early years model remains.

The international sharing of ideas on early years services means that some countries have sought to move from a split to an integrated model. New Zealand (Dalli, 2008) and the UK (Campbell-Barr, 2015) offer examples of countries that have sought to restructure their early years services to develop a more integrated approach in more recent times, albeit with arguable levels of success. In New Zealand, which began a process of integration in 1986, the approach has not only been about co-locating services within one government department, but also about developing a revised framework for workforce training, whereby teachers represent core staff (Moss, 2006). In the UK, since 1998, there have been various initiatives to develop a more integrated early years model, such as developing one curriculum stage for children from birth to five and co-locating services in one government department. However, the UK's legacy of a split model is still evident within workforce requirements, whereby there is a range of different professional roles and training requirements dependent on where an individual is working (see Chapter 2).

The Workforce

In analysing the question of who is an early years professional, the split model can equate to split training requirements, both in regard to the focus of training and the qualification levels that are required. For example, across Europe, it is possible to see that those working with older children are more likely to require an 'education' focused qualification and those working with younger children, a 'care' focused qualification (Commission/EACEA/Eurydice/Eurostat, 2014). Those working with older children are more likely to be referred to as teachers or educators, whilst those working with younger children are referred to as child-carers, nursery workers and nursery nurses (Adams, 2008; McGillivray, 2008). Job titles inevitably vary within different countries, reflecting the range of services that can exist (Urban et al., 2012). The variations create inconsistencies in children's experiences, as well as a confused array of terminology on how to refer to those who work in early years services. Moloney (2010a), researching in Ireland, identified amongst a sample of 56 participants, 20 different terms for referring to their job roles (Figure 1.1). Whilst the early years professional landscape has changed since Moloney undertook her research, the list of terms is representative of the complex array of job titles that exist for those working in early years services in different international contexts.

Terms to refer to early years professionals come with connotations, whereby words such as teacher can imply a transmission role and those encompassing nurse imply a more health focused role (Adams, 2008; Oberhuemer, 2005). To some extent, the terms will reflect the different expectations of the professionals and this will be related to the role and purpose that the early years services are seen to serve (as discussed above).

Practitioner, nursery assistant, childcare assistant, childcare worker, early years worker, crèche worker, crèche assistant, educarer, key worker, childcare staff, pre-school assistant, pre-school tutor, pre-school worker, pre-school leader, nursery worker, playgroup worker, playgroup leader, teacher, Montessori teacher and Montessori assistant

Figure 1.1 Overview of terminology used to describe the ECCE worker
Reproduced from Moloney (2010a: Figure 3, p. 177).

Inevitably, in considering a cross-European perspective (as well as beyond Europe) the question of terminology also raises issues of translation. In many European countries the term pedagogue is used to refer to those working in early years services, but the term pedagogue has an uneasy relationship within the English language (Moss, 2006). Often pedagogue is translated as teacher, but it actually has a much more holistic interpretation (Moss, 2006). During my own time living in Hungary, I was often told how the Hungarian term '*óvodapedagógus*' was typically translated as kindergarten (*óvoda*) teacher (*pedagógus*), but that actually the role of a person working in a kindergarten was better associated with the word 'educator'. The word teacher (*tanár*) is not used as an *óvodapedagógus* does not teach; instead there is a different philosophy that adopts a play-based approach to support children's development (Nagy Varga et al., 2015). The term teacher is regarded as akin to that of a school teacher who transmits knowledge (Oberhuemer, 2005). The example of Hungary illustrates that one aspect of who is an early years professional is that of establishing the profession as distinct to that of teaching. Therefore, in considering the knowledge and skills of early years professionals there is an argument to be made that they are distinct from the knowledge and skills of a teacher (see Chapter 2).

QUESTION

How would you describe your professional identity? What job title do you have? Is this care or education focused? Would you change your job title in any way?

What is a Professional?

The discussion presented so far has illustrated the complexities of who is an early years professional. Definitions are tied to constructions of the role and purpose of early years services, whilst being deeply entwined with constructions of gender and who is best placed to care for and educate young children. Understanding who is an early years professional risks becoming a series of binaries, such as care or education, male or female, and this is constraining as binaries can exclude some people from being identified as an early years professional. I do not ascribe to the binaries, particularly those surrounding gender, and I hope that I have demonstrated that within the term 'early years' there is a plethora of different early years professionals that will reflect the context that they are in. However, whilst I have explored interpretations of 'early years', it is equally important to consider what is meant by the term 'professional'. Considering what professional means begins a process of thinking about both a knowledge-base and who determines the knowledge-base.

Concepts of what it means to be a professional have been debated from many theoretical perspectives (Brock, 2013), with many of the debates being concerned with an identifiable knowledge-base and a sense of dedication and/or responsibility to the profession (Adams, 2008; Brock, 2013; Dalli, 2008; Urban et al., 2012). However, the process of identifying a knowledge-base has two core questions:

1   What is the knowledge required for working in the early years?
2   Who decides what is the knowledge required for working in the early years?

These two questions are clearly closely related and this is well demonstrated in discussions on early years professionalism.

As outlined above, the interest in the social welfare function of early years services by policy makers has resulted in increased scrutiny of both services and those who work in them. The scrutiny has been more than just a question of what is the role of early years services, but also about how policy makers can ensure that role is fulfilled. Policy makers have therefore been concerned with professionalism as it has consequences for the success of early years policy objectives. However, from a policy perspective, the question of what is the early years knowledge-base becomes one of what is the knowledge required to fulfil the early years policy objectives. For example, the knowledge required to be an 'education' member of staff would potentially be different to that of a 'care' member of staff. Knowledge is, therefore, tied to understanding the social purpose of the profession, but as illustrated, there can be different perspectives on the purpose of early years services.

Recognising that the early years knowledge-base will be tied to understanding the social purpose of the profession demonstrates that professionalism is both individual and social – the knowledge an individual requires to fulfil their social responsibility. Further, the interplay between the individual and the social demonstrates that professionalism is more than just a question of a knowledge-base, but about what is done with the knowledge, how it is applied (Winch, 2014). The question of knowledge and knowledge application is something that I will return to throughout the book, but what is key here is that the interest by policy makers in early years professionalism risks there being just one story of what it is to be an early years professional. As policy makers want early years professionals to achieve particular objectives there is a risk of technocratic and narrow concepts of professionalism. The technocratic professionalism represents a model of:

We (society) want to achieve X, therefore we require professionals with knowledge Y to achieve this.

Working with young children becomes like a cake recipe, a mere question of adding the right ingredients at the right times and left to bake to perfection (see Chapter 2).

Technocratic models of professionalism become about identifiable attributes, such as a list of knowledge and skills against which individuals are to demonstrate their competence (Urban et al., 2012).

The decision as to what knowledge and skills are required is presented as a top-down bureaucratic process, which results in the views of the early years workforce going unheard (Brock, 2013; Dalli, 2008; Osgood, 2012). Bottom-up perspectives that come from those working with young children are identified as being more ethical, capturing a wider concept of what it means to work with young children than those of competence profiles (Brock, 2013; Dahlberg and Moss, 2005; Oberhuemer, 2005; Osgood, 2012; Taggart, 2016). The bottom-up concept of early years professionalism therefore encompasses features that might not necessarily be identifiable, but are nonetheless important. For example, the lasting legacy of the Romantic Movement has been identified as important to those who work in early years services, but is not necessarily captured in technocratic models of professionalism that favour identifiable attributes.

The top-down process is one that has been identified as being counter to professionalism as it denies professional autonomy and the ability for the profession to determine its own knowledge-base (Osgood, 2006; Simpson, 2010). The notion of the top-down model positions early years professionals as passive recipients of policy, rather than active agents in their own professional identity formation. However, research with those who work with young children demonstrates that they have ideas as to what it means to be a professional and that standards and regulation can provide opportunities and a legitimate knowledge-base that individuals can identify with, thus contributing to their professional identity (Miller, 2008). The notion of top-down and bottom-up does not have to be a question of either/or, because (as will be demonstrated throughout the book) the knowledge and skills required for working in the early years are multiple and varied. Professional identity can be about both professional standards and personal perspectives, explaining why no two professionals are the same.

━━━━━━━━━━ **QUESTION** ━━━━━━━━━━

What are the knowledge and skills that you think are important for being an early years professional?

Conclusion

The different perspectives on early years professionalism reflect that it is a much debated area (Dalli, 2008). The question of who is an early years professional is multiple, varied and contested, influenced by the cultural context and understandings of the role of early years services. Historical perspectives demonstrate the changing understandings of early years services and those who work in them, but for early years professionals they become a meeting point for different concepts on how to care for and educate young children. For example, whilst romantic concepts of childhood, combined with a maternal discourse, have influenced a gendered construction of who is an early years professional, post-structural perspectives have challenged hetero-normativity, with early years professionals negotiating between these different perspectives.

Interpretations of early years professionalism are both social and individual. Throughout the chapter, it has been evident that the social has been important in shaping understandings of early years professionalism. Socio-cultural histories, including those related to policy intervention, shape understandings of early years services and those that work in them, but individual interpretations and experiences also interplay. The combination of the social and the individual is further evident in how professionalism will be about individual knowledge and skills, applied to fulfil the social responsibility of caring for and educating young children. Thus despite dominant cultural and/or policy perspectives on early years services, individuals will engage with them in varying ways. So the question of who is an early years professional becomes a series of questions on what is the role of early years services and what is the knowledge required to fulfil this role – questions to be returned to throughout the book.

CHAPTER SUMMARY

- History provides insights that facilitate an understanding of present narratives on early years services.
- Early years services are cultural sites, representing deeply embedded socio-cultural ideas on how best to care for and educate young children.
- Romantic concepts of childhood have combined with a maternal discourse to influence a gendered construction of who is an early years professional.
- Early years services represent a meeting of care and education and countries have different ways of conceptualising early years services as care, education or educare.
- Post-structural perspectives question dominant discourses (such as hetero-normativity) and question the power dynamics in defining who is an early years professional.
- Professionalism is about the knowledge required to work with young children and how to apply it.
- Who is an early years professional is complex, multiple and varied.

FURTHER READING

Moss, P. (2006). 'Structures, understandings and discourses: possibilities for re-envisioning the early childhood worker', *Contemporary Issues in Early Childhood*, 7(1), 30–41.

This is a helpful discussion of the challenges of a split early years model and the implications for understanding who is an early years professional.

Early Education: https://www.early-education.org.uk/extended-history-early-education

The British Association for Early Childhood Education offer a range of resources for those working in the early years, but this particular page adds to the brief history presented here in this chapter.

2

QUALITY IN THE EARLY YEARS AND EARLY YEARS TRAINING

Quality has become an accepted prefix to early years services and I do not dispute the importance of quality (why would society want anything other than quality early years services for young children?). However, in this chapter I am interested in how quality is conceptualised and the consequences that this has for early years professionals. I begin by briefly outlining how understandings of the quality of early years services have developed and the prevailing discourse of 'quality and high returns' within early years policy rationales. I consider how the interest in quality has resulted in increased scrutiny of those who work in early years services, but identify that despite the common international interest in quality, the international early years workforce is characterised by divergence. I contemplate the different training models that exist for the early years workforce in different national contexts, before going on to critically explore the purpose of early years training. I consider whether training is about personal professional development, meeting the needs of the labour market, or a more holistic interpretation of acquiring the knowledge, skills and attitudes appropriate for the context.

Quality and High Returns

Supra-national organisations such as the OECD (OECD, 2011, 2015b) and the European Commission (European Commission, 2014) advocate the importance of 'quality' early years services as a **social investment** strategy for individual countries. The emphasis on 'quality' is the result of an evolution of research into early years services. Fenech (2011) explores how research into the quality of early years services has encompassed considering the effects of maternal and non-maternal care on child development, identifying features of quality services, and recognising that the context of the child (notably their family circumstances) was important in analysing the effects of quality early years services. The research reflects understandings of early years services as meeting the dual objectives of supporting maternal employment and equality of access to the educational advantages of early years services for children (see Chapter 1).

The identifying of features of quality has been particularly significant in developing an increased scrutiny of early years professionals. However, it is important to recognise that the scrutiny of the workforce has been shaped by the way in which quality has been identified within research. Positivistic research paradigms, which approach social research as a scientific exercise, whereby logic and mathematical proof offer valid data, consider quality to be measurable. Fuelled by modernistic perspectives of society that reflect a rational and objective view of the world, 'the focus is on creating a knowable world, grounded in scientific evidence' (Campbell-Barr and Leeson, 2016: 22). Beyond the clear question as to whether it is possible to measure quality, it is important to recognise that within modernist frameworks, measurements of quality will be determined by the outcomes that are socially ascribed onto early years services. As such, understandings of good quality early years services will be those that achieve the socially desired outcomes. If the desired outcomes are related to child development (as they frequently are), definitions of quality, and the identification of indicators of quality, will be the attributes of early years services that produce the best child outcomes. Therefore, for those working in early years services, 'quality' staff will be those who can demonstrate an improvement in child development.

As research began to identify the features of quality that could contribute to child outcomes, it was also possible to identify where quality early years services had the most impact. Research that analysed the context of the child identified that children from socio-economically deprived backgrounds could gain the most from quality services. Quality early years services could, therefore, support a child's development, but particularly for children from disadvantaged backgrounds (Campbell-Barr and Leeson, 2016).

The social investment function of early years services is exemplified by economic research. Human capital perspectives, whereby investments in early years services are regarded as an investment in the foundations of children's development and their later productivity as an adult, have become popular amongst international organisations as a rationale for investing in services. The human capital perspective presents early years services as a wise investment as the monies invested will be more than saved by a reduction in economic spending in the future, such as reduced additional educational needs support, alongside a more productive workforce on the children entering adulthood. The result is that the economic rationale of invest now (in young children and their education) and save later has become normative in understandings of early years services (Campbell-Barr, 2012). However, the economic argument is dependent on being able to measure both quality and child outcomes, as well as ascribe economic value to those outcomes. Whilst again there are questions of what can and cannot be measured (and economically assessed), there is also a concern that children become valued on the basis of their outcomes, many of which are only assessed on their entering adulthood.

More recently, the positivistic and economic assessments of quality have been joined by developments in neuroscience. Wastell and White (2012) explore the increasing influence of neuroscience in informing policy decisions. The policy objective to improve the lives of disadvantaged children has inevitably drawn upon the economic debates outlined above, but now neuroscience research presents early years services as a now or never intervention. The Allen (2011) report has become synonymous with the use of neuroscience by policy makers due to the provocative front cover of the brains of two three year olds, one appearing larger than the other and being labelled 'normal', while the second, smaller brain, is labelled 'extreme neglect'. Whilst the cover presumes the reader to be an expert in understanding neurological scans, the report is illustrative of a scientific identification of the importance of early intervention to support prescriptive normative child development. I am not looking to challenge the neuroscientific evidence as there are compelling features to the research, and I recognise that I am not an expert in neuroscience. However, I do think it is important to recognise that research on early child development and early years services has a lasting legacy in shaping understandings of early years professionals. In many respects, those who work in the early years are now the answer to everything – the development of the child neurologically, socially, emotionally and economically.

Despite the growth in socio-economic and neurological perspectives on early years services, there is another wave of research that seeks to open up debates on interpretations of quality and their consequences for understanding child development and early years professionals. The story of early intervention, coupled with that of quality and economic returns, presents particular stories of early years services, early years professionals and children. There is a strong deficit model of children evident in how they are valued for what they are to become, not what they are (see Chapter 5). The deficit model of child development is coupled with concerns about the potentially limiting understanding of early years practice, whereby professionals are tasked with creating the right child and achieving the prescribed outcomes (Dahlberg and Moss, 2005).

The role of the early years professional risks being framed by the social investment strategy, whereby professionals are tasked with 'narrowing the gap' between the attainment and development of children from different socio-economic backgrounds. Thus, a more critical perspective of quality early years services is about opening up alternative stories, whilst also highlighting the power structures involved in determining which stories are heard (Moss, 2014a).

Training and Quality

The previous chapter, on 'what does it mean to be a professional in the early years?', has already outlined how changes in understandings of the role of early years services have had consequences for what it means to be an early years professional. Research into the quality of early years services provides another layer to understanding professionalism, because the synergy between quality and the early years workforce has led to questions of training – in regard to its focus, level and model. Whilst training cannot be seen as a prerequisite for professionalism, the initial training of the early years workforce can be identified as an aspect of professional development. Consequently, there is a complex relationship between interpretations of the role of early years services, constructions of quality, the importance of initial training for quality and understandings of professionalism. However, as will be explored in this section, the prevailing influence of modernist approaches means that often there is a focus on the structural features of training, rather than a more holistic approach of considering what training should consist of and how best it can support the preparation of early years professionals.

Research into the quality of early years services has tended to focus on the level of training as a measurable proxy for the workforce. Higher levels of training are routinely demonstrated as central to the overall quality of early years services. The English based Effective Provision of Preschool Education (EPPE) study has demonstrated associations between staff qualifications and quality (Sylva et al., 2004). In essence, higher qualified members of the early years workforce are identified as having more knowledge of developmentally appropriate practice and provide richer learning environments (see Fukkink and Lont, 2007). The result is that associations between the quality of the early years workforce and the overall quality of early years services are widely accepted (Jones, 2014), with correlation research demonstrating the training of the workforce as the cornerstone of quality (Fukkink and Lont, 2007).

Quality has therefore become synonymous with the workforce (Urban, 2008), with training being the tool to create a quality workforce. Whilst there is a given logic to the importance of the workforce for the quality of early years services, this does not mean there is a consensus on what training is required of those who work with young children. For example, the EPPE study demonstrated the importance of graduate level qualifications, but due to the time at which the study was conducted, graduates were concentrated in the maintained (state) sector and therefore had teaching qualifications. Whilst graduate level qualifications have been introduced for the private, voluntary and independent (PVI) sectors, they remain different from those of the maintained sector. In England, those working in the maintained sector as teachers are required to hold a degree with Qualified Teacher Status (QTS), but the commitment to have a degree member of staff in all (PVI) settings was removed under the austerity measures of the Conservative–Liberal Democrat government (2010–2015). The result is that whilst degrees are a requirement for those in the maintained sector, for PVI settings, Leaders are expected to have a Level 3 qualification, with half of all other staff at Level 2.

Degrees for PVI settings are popular (see Table 2.1, where group-based and childminders represent PVI settings), but they have been clouded by debates on terminology from the Early Years Professional Status that was introduced in 2006 and the subsequent Early Years Initial Teacher Training Status introduced in 2014. The former raised questions as to understandings of professionalism and the latter has fuelled debates in regard to the inequity in status and conditions between 'teachers' working in different sectors (Georgeson and Payler, 2014). As demonstrated by Table 2.2 (see next page), pay levels vary between the sectors, with those in the maintained sector (Nursery and Reception) receiving the highest salaries. Questions of inequity are important when considering early years professionals (irrespective of qualification type), particularly given that in

Table 2.1 Percentage of staff qualifications in England by sector

Qualification	Group-based	Nursery	Reception	Childminders
No UK Early Years qualification	7%	6%	8%	17%
At least Level 1	90%	87%	87%	78%
At least Level 2	89%	85%	84%	74%
At least Level 3	79%	77%	74%	69%
At least Level 4	19%	37%	45%	16%
At least Level 5	14%	32%	41%	11%
At least Level 6	10%	29%	39%	8%
Other	1%	–	–	4%
Don't know	1%	5%	4%	2%
Refused	–	–	–	–
Unweighted base size	11,666	2,802	1,750	1,444

Data obtained from Childcare and Early Years Providers Survey 2016, Tables SFR 09/2017, Public et al. (2017)
© Crown copyright 2017. Reproduced under the Open Government Licence v3.0 www.nationalarchives.gov.uk/doc/open-government-licence/version/3/

Table 2.2 Average pay by setting and seniority of staff (rate per hour)

Staff member	Group-based	Reception	Nursery
Senior manager / head teacher/Early Years Coordinator	£11.20	£24.80	£25.80
Non-senior staff	£8.00	£13.00	£11.90

Public et al. (2017) © Crown copyright 2017, reproduced under the Open Government License v3.0 www.nationalarchives.gov.uk/doc/open-government-licence/version/3/

the English context staff will all be delivering the same curriculum (the Early Years Foundation Stage). However, what is pertinent here is whether the different qualifications have consequences for the quality of the early years workforce and the quality of early years services.

Within England, settings are inspected by Ofsted and given a quality grading of Outstanding, Good, Inadequate or Requires Improvement. The quality gradings are not without their problems (see Campbell-Barr and Leeson, 2016). Public et al. (2017) explored the relationship between qualifications and Ofsted gradings and found a clear pattern that group-based providers with higher Ofsted ratings were more likely to have a highly qualified senior manager, with the same pattern being true of non-managers (although less defined). Determining a similar pattern for the maintained sector, however, is problematic as there is an expectation that staff will have degrees. Whilst the data support the earlier research findings of associations between qualifications and quality, there is little to indicate what it is that a qualification does to support the quality of provision.

International variations in training

The English early years model is one that highlights the complexities of what a quality early years workforce might look like, but the complexities are not unique to England. Internationally there are examples of where there are different qualification requirements depending on the age of children a professional is working with and whether services are classified as being care or education focused (see Chapter 1). However, behind the questions as to whether initial training should focus on care or education and at what level it should be, the distinctions between the qualifications for working with different ages of children raise questions as to the age focus of initial early years training. For example, within French preschools (*écoles maternelles*), staff are required to hold a Master's qualification. However, the Master's training is combined with those going on to work in primary schools, with concerns that it is the needs of the primary school teacher that form the prime focus of the training (Garnier, 2011). French day nurseries (crèches) employ primarily auxiliary nursery nurses, who have an upper secondary education qualification, along with educators and nursery nurses who have a Bachelor's degree. The French model therefore raises some interesting questions in regard to training and quality.

<hr/>

QUESTIONS

Are the training needs of early years professionals the same as those of primary school teachers?

Do those working with younger children (birth to three) require a different form and/or content of training to those working in preschools?

Should qualifications for working in the early years be education, care or educare focused?

<hr/>

It is important to note that France is not the only country to divide training requirements depending on where a person is working and with what age children. Arguably, the French model offers an example of where nurseries have a range of staff with different qualifications to form a rich and varied workforce. Whilst having combinations of staff offers one potential solution to the question of what form of training is best (instead early years settings compensate by having a range), the debates on the structure of early years training are evidence of the complex history of early years services in Europe (see Chapter 1) and the lasting legacy of a division between childcare for young children and early education for preschool children. However, there is evidence of countries that have sought to identify alternative initial early years training structures.

Initial training models

New Zealand, following a policy initiative to integrate care and education services (see Chapter 1), developed an integrated training model in 1988 as a three-year degree. The initiative provided a training pathway that paralleled those working in primary education (Dalli, 2008). Within the revised model, the term teacher is used across early years and primary school professionals, although pay parity was not present until 2002. Whilst the New Zealand model is heralded as a great success, it is also one that identifies the challenges of integrating different historical, philosophical and organisational constructs of early years services (Dalli, 2008; Moss, 2006). As Andrew (2015) writes from the Australian context, where the integration of care and education staff is less developed, integrating care and education staff involves integrating two very different philosophies of how to work with young children. Arguably, it is the different philosophies between early education and primary school that also created a problem within the French training model.

In Denmark, the philosophy underpinning the training of those who will work in early years services is distinct, as is the structuring of the training. Initial early years training involves a three-and-a-half year Bachelor's degree that can enable an individual to work in early years services, youth services and services for those with disabilities (Moss, 2006). Students undertake a combination of basic (generic) training, followed by a specialist year, combining both practical and theoretical elements (Jensen et al., 2010). The Danish model is one of a social pedagogue, which signifies more than a model of bringing together care and education. The Danish philosophy is grounded in democratic perspectives, representing a relational and holistic approach to working with children. Learning, care and upbringing are interconnected facets of the professional role (Moss, 2006). Whilst not all Danish professionals will have a Bachelor's degree, they represent the majority of staff (Jensen, 2015). The philosophy of the social pedagogue means that it offers something more than just combining the training of preschool teachers with primary teachers or adopting an educare approach as is evident in other countries.

The examples of New Zealand and Denmark illustrate that training models are more than a question of structure, such as the overall qualification level, which age groups are being focused upon and whether training is focused on education, care or educare. There is a far deeper philosophical perspective that underpins early years training models that will have been derived from historical developments in early years services and social constructions of the role and purpose of early years services (see Chapter 1). However, as the example of New Zealand clearly illustrates, policy interventions can lead to changes in both the structural and philosophical approach to early years training. Further, countries that are held up as examples of good practice, such as Denmark, are not immune to policy pressures to change their approach to training. The interest in the quality of early years services and those who work in them means that training requirements are often subject to continued reforms, as is well illustrated by England in the discussion above.

The Purpose of Training

The relationship between initial training and quality demonstrates that one purpose of early years training is to develop the quality of early years services. As discussed, the definition of quality will be tied to conceptions of the role and purpose of early years services. As such, early years services that seek to educate children (for example) will require staff who can provide for, and support children's education. Initial training and later professional development opportunities will therefore look to develop the knowledge, skills and attitudes required of a person to fulfil the role of early years services. In contexts where there is a high level of policy interest in early years services and prescriptive policy objectives as to the role of early years services, the professional role can become tied to the policy objectives (see Chapter 1). Professionalism becomes a process of applying the right techniques at the right time to achieve the desired objectives (Dahlberg and Moss, 2005).

However, early years professionals are not only the objects of policy as they will negotiate other demands in shaping their professionalism, including the demands of the labour market. The demands of the labour market will, to an extent, interplay with the policy context, whereby national legislative requirements will dictate the demands of the labour market. For example, there are formulaic aspects to applying for a job as an early years professional, reflected in requirements to provide a criminal record check, references, identity check, etc. (Powell, 2010). Further, in market-based early years models where there is a dominance of private sector providers, the knowledge and skills required may also include features relating to managing a business. Economic drivers for a sustainable and viable business require consistency and stability, whereby the labour market demands more of the same, rather than innovation and change (Urban et al., 2012). Consistency and stability relate to notions of predictability whereby both the labour market and policy makers require certainty that economic and policy objectives will be met. Within such contexts the knowledge and skills that help to secure stability and consistency will be favoured over other potential forms of knowledge and skills. The risk being that professionalism becomes a formulaic response to the conditions of the labour market.

The role of the labour market in shaping professionalism also relates to wider debates on employability. The earlier discussion of the influence of socio-economics on early years services is not solely about the consequences that they have for children and their learning. Whilst early years services are identified as the foundations to lifelong learning, wider debates on lifelong learning illustrate that learning has become orientated towards the labour market (Vandenbroeck et al., 2013). Framed by broader conceptions of globalisation and **personal economic responsibility**, individuals undertake training to secure employment. Thus within this framework initial early years training is for the purpose of finding later employment.

Whilst there is an inevitability that individuals undertake training in order to find later employment, they will also want to develop their individual knowledge and skills. The individual should not be confused with personal (see Chapter 6), instead the focus here is on individual competence. As touched upon in Chapter 1, the term competence has been open to much debate, because it is often associated with technocratic professionalism (Vandenbroeck et al., 2013), reflecting a simplistic process of acquiring the 'right' competences, with an assumption that competence can be viewed, observed and assessed in objective ways. Competence models are criticised for failing to support a more holistic approach to professionalism, being overly individualised and implying an end goal of becoming competent (Urban et al., 2012). However, competence is something of a vague term with a variable meaning (Strohmer and Mischo, 2016). In England, competence is often understood as 'good enough', whereby a competent person is someone who has met the prescribed standards (Cameron and Miller, 2016). However, within continental Europe, the term competence has a more holistic interpretation, 'referring not just to knowledge or skills, but also the ability to successfully meet complex demands in a particular context' (Cameron and Miller, 2016: 103). Thus whilst competence can be focused on the acquisition of knowledge and skills, there is recognition that it will also be about developing dispositions, attitudes and emotional responses (Urban et al., 2011). Further, initial early years training is not about reaching an end goal of being 'competent', but a fluctuating process of developing a self-concept of competence (Strohmer and Mischo, 2016).

Combining Theory and Practice in Initial Training

In accepting that competence is a complex term and not a fixed state, the purpose of initial early years training becomes the starting point of a journey in acquiring the knowledge and skills to be applied to the context. Whilst subsequent chapters look in detail at the knowledge and skills required for the early years context, it is important to establish that within early years initial training models there is a general acceptance that the process of acquiring knowledge and skills requires both theory and practice. Amongst early years professionals, there is often recognition of the importance of children's experiential learning, but professionals themselves will also learn through experience (Hedges and Cullen, 2005). Initial early years training therefore combines practical and experiential learning alongside the theoretical, but as I will return to many times in this book, the relationship between these different forms of learning creates intricate and multifaceted knowledge relationships.

One of the complexities in the relationship between theory and practice is whether one is more important than the other. Important might not be quite the right word, as really it is about whether there is a balance between theory and practice in developing the required professional knowledge and skills. The balance between the theoretical and the practical has been shaped by evolutions in early years initial training, not least the shift towards higher levels of training in support of quality services. Whilst theory and practice are identified as being entwined within an applied profession such as the early years (for example, knowledge of child development needs to be applied in practice if a professional is to support a child to develop), the shift towards higher qualifications in support of quality early years services has seen a trend in early years initial training being located within universities. The move to university level professional training is not unique to the early years (for example, nursing and social work have seen similar trends). It is also worth stating that there are many complex debates about knowledge and skills within university contexts that are beyond the scope of this book, but that nonetheless have an impact on the relationship between theory and practice within early years university level training. One of the consequences of a move towards higher levels of training for early years professionals is that practice-based and experiential learning is often identified as inferior (Karlsson, 2015). Academic knowledge is privileged as a more robust form of knowledge (something that I will challenge in later chapters), particularly within university contexts.

The devaluing of practice-based and experiential learning is set against a historical context of university courses being grounded in academic disciplines (see Furlong and Whitty, 2017, for a fuller discussion). However, within practical professions, such as early years, the privileging of academic knowledge is challenged. The earlier discussion on lifelong learning has demonstrated that training has become orientated to the labour market and employability. The practical aspects of working with young children and meeting the needs of the labour market have seen an emphasis on practical training and a devaluing of academic knowledge for early years professionalism. For example, in Sweden, changes in early years initial training have been through various iterations including a shift towards university-based training and subsequent criticism of academic knowledge being too abstract and not grounded in practice (Karlsson, 2015). In Denmark, there were similar criticisms following initial early years training reforms and now students spend about one third of their time in practice (Jensen, 2015; Onnismaa et al., 2015). Time in practice in the Danish model is identified as providing opportunities for applying and creating knowledge in practice as students move towards mastering the profession (Jensen, 2015). The time in practice therefore reflects that knowledge acquisition and creation are not confined to theory.

Onnismaa et al. (2015) outline the Finnish model of combining theory and practice, whereby students progressively take on more responsibility within their practical training. Initial practical placements begin with students observing children and the learning environment. A second stage of placements involves planning, implementation and evaluation, whereby students are required to develop drama or nature and mathematics sessions that they deliver to children and then evaluate through both a dual supervision model (one practice-based and one university-based supervisor) and peer (fellow student) review. The final stage of practice sees students taking on holistic responsibility within the early years setting.

Hungary adopts a very similar model of students taking on progressively more responsibility in practice over the three years of their academic study to become a kindergarten pedagogue (Oberhuemer et al., 2010). Embedded within the training is a connection between taught aspects of pedagogical practice, such as music and singing, which students then apply in their practice in the kindergarten. However, my own research in Hungary has demonstrated that one of the challenges of developing practice-based training is the requirement for students to be assessed (Campbell-Barr, 2017a). Practice becomes focused on the need to assess students in particular tasks, such as the singing or drama activity. The structure of the day within the kindergarten will therefore reflect the need for the student to be assessed, rather than how a student responds to the needs of a child and their emerging interests (Campbell-Barr, 2017a). Thus whilst there is a complex relationship between theory and practice within early years initial professional training, the relationship is made all the more challenging when the purpose of initial training is to pass the assessments.

Amongst those training to work in early years services there is often a favouring of the practical elements of training. In some contexts, this reflects the historical evolution of services (see Chapter 1), whereby services have evolved from supporting women entering employment, to the recent emphasis on quality as a social welfare strategy. For example, in England, where there has been a historical lack of political intervention in early years services, there was little interest in the training of early years professionals. However, the increased interest in the social welfare potential of early years services, along with an appreciation for the importance of quality and the role of the workforce in delivering quality early years services, has seen more emphasis (and debate) placed on training. The historical position of early years services is one where experience was enough to enable a person to work with children, offering one explanation as to why there is a favouring of experiential learning (Colley, 2006; Vincent and Braun, 2011). The displacement of theory is not necessarily a rejection of it, but a reflection of a convoluted relationship with the history of early years services (McGillivray, 2008).

The favouring of practical training within the English model is further complicated by fluctuating policy commitments to have (or not) a graduate trained workforce across all early years services (as discussed earlier). With early years settings in the PVI sectors not being required to have a graduate leader, most members of the workforce will undertake vocational training, with an emphasis on practice. The second explanation for why there is a favouring of practical elements of training amongst early years professionals could be that many of the workforce have undertaken vocational (practical) training. However, even in Hungary, where there is a long history of degree (graduate) level training for those working in kindergartens, students still valued the practical elements of their training more than the theoretical (Campbell-Barr, 2017a). In very simplistic terms, for the students I worked with in Hungary, it was because the time in practice was real (they had experienced it), but also it gave them time with children – the people who they had chosen to and wanted to work with. Undoubtedly there are challenging aspects to working with children (as I will return to in later chapters), but surely the driving force for anyone undertaking initial early years training is to be with children.

Conclusion

The discussion on the relationship between theory and practice demonstrates many of the key themes within this chapter on quality and training in the early years. Firstly, recognition of the importance of quality early years services has resulted in an increased scrutiny of early years professionals, particularly how they are trained. Both policy makers and the labour market want a degree of predictability in what early years professionals will do (and the outcomes they will achieve) when working in early years services. Training therefore becomes the process by which to develop the 'right' kind of early years professional, with assessment being the tool with which to judge an individual's competence in being the 'right' kind of professional. Within practical training, the assessments focus on the performing of particular tasks as a form of technical practice (Dahlberg and Moss, 2005). Practical assessments have become a necessary component for determining a student's success in becoming the right kind of professional, but they risk constraining professionalism to a performance of tasks rather than a more holistic interpretation.

Students value their time in practice as it provides time to engage with children. However, learning to be with children is challenging and far more than a simple process of applying the right knowledge at the right time or performing tasks in the presumed correct way. Working with children is a complex combination of knowledge, skills and attitudes and these will be developed via both theory and practice. However, it is also important to recognise that the knowledge, skills and attitudes required for the context of working in the early years will not only be shaped by the needs of policy makers and the workforce, but will also reflect deeply engrained views as to the philosophical thinking behind care, education and educare. Early years services in different cultural context will have different perspectives on what knowledge, skills and attitudes underpin early years professionalism and to what extent there are differences depending on the age of the child that a person is working with or the type of service. In the next chapter, I explore some of the intricacies of how people come to know how to work with young children.

CHAPTER SUMMARY

- There is increased political interest in the quality of early years services due to a growing recognition of the role quality services can play in supporting children's early development.
- Definitions of quality are often framed by positivist approaches that view quality as a measurable entity. Measurements of quality are determined by the desired outcomes of early years services. Quality risks being restricted to narrow definitions of the role of early years services.
- Heightened interest in the quality of early years services has resulted in an increased scrutiny of those who work in early years services. Professional roles risk being shaped by policy objectives of the role of early years.
- Despite a global interest in the quality of early years services and those who work in them, the early years workforce is characterised by divergence when looking at international models.
- Training to work in early years services involves the development of the knowledge, skills and attitudes required for the context via both theory and practice.

FURTHER READING

Campbell-Barr, V. (2018). 'The silencing of the knowledge-base in early childhood education and care professionalism', *International Journal of Early Years Education*, 26(1): 75–89.

This paper highlights the theoretical challenges in forming a knowledge-base for early years professionals.

The Early Childhood Workforce Initiative: www.earlychildhoodworkforce.org/

The Early Childhood Workforce Initiative focuses on those who work with children and families around the world. The website offers case studies and materials from a range of different countries, illustrating that early years professionals can encompass home visitors, preschool staff, community health workers and those who are there to support the professionals.

3

KNOWLEDGES IN THE EARLY YEARS

In this chapter I want to consider what knowledge is, how it is constructed and how it is applied. Considering all three questions is potentially challenging as the answer to one question will stray into the answering of another. The complexities of exploring knowledge are further confounded by the challenges and critiques that have been made of knowledge, particularly what constitutes professional knowledge within the early years. To help overcome some of these challenges, I want to focus on knowledges. I see knowledge as plural, as I believe that knowledge comes in different forms, with different structures, and is acquired in different ways. I do not see the process of coming to know as being one where there is an end goal that can be reached. Rather, I see knowing as an ongoing and fluid process; but I recognise that this is shaped by my own view of what knowledge is. Therefore, within this chapter, I consider the different forms of knowledge that can exist, how they are evaluated and how they come together to inform professional practice, but frame this within a broader discussion of what is knowledge.

What is Knowledge?

The question of what is knowledge is something of a perennial topic that goes back as far as philosophers such as Plato. Concepts of knowledge have changed with time, being debated and analysed from many theoretical perspectives. Broadly, knowledge has a history of being positioned as science or philosophy (Young and Muller, 2007), both of which have their own process for determining what knowledge is. Questions of the nature of knowledge impose **epistemological** perspectives as to the methods and protocols for establish something is 'true' (Furlong and Whitty, 2017). Epistemology is the theory of knowledge, concerned with its methods, validity and reach. For example, within the sciences, the notion of an experiment to prove a hypothesis is deemed to provide an objective and accurate assessment of knowledge. Philosophical traditions have a more interpretive approach and have been more concerned with what knowledge consists of, what we can know, the limits of knowledge and even whether it is possible to know at all. Such philosophical questions might leave you, as a reader, thinking 'I don't *know* what she's talking about', so you might be pleased to hear that I am not about to embark on a philosophical exploration of knowledge. Questions surrounding the nature of knowledge have been, and continue to be, debated, but I want to focus upon *what knowledge is* when considered within the context of a profession, such as early years.

Knowledge is central to a profession, whereby professionalism is the application of expert and specialised knowledge. There is a danger of universalising knowledge when analysing it in relation to a particular profession such as early years, due to the potential for lists of knowledge to be created (see Chapter 2 and the discussion on technocratic professionalism). Therefore, the focus on knowledges is about appreciating the multiplicity of the early years knowledge-base, with later sections in this chapter (and later chapters) focusing on how knowledges come together to inform professional practice.

A knowledge-base is central to a profession as it is what distinguishes between a profession and an occupation. Arguably there is something of a hierarchy in professions in regard to the identification of a knowledge-base, from those with well-established disciplinary cores, with associated professional bodies (such as doctors and the British Medical Council), to questions of semi-professions and new professions. However, debating what is (or is not) a profession does little to consider the question of knowledge (Young and Muller, 2014). In many respects, the question of what the knowledge-base is for early years professionals has eluded consideration in favour of questioning meanings of 'professional' and 'professionalism' and concern as to the processes for determining professional knowledge. Therefore, my interest is in bringing knowledge back into discussions of early years professionalism.

The example of medicine as an established profession, with an established disciplinary core, provides a basis with which to consider what knowledge is within early years professionalism. A disciplinary core implies that there is a foundation on which a professional can know something to be true. Disciplines represent different branches of knowledge, with particular rules, methods and boundaries that determine knowledge.

Knowledge is tied to the process of understanding how the knowledge was determined and validated. Medicine illustrates how the process of determining and validating knowledge has historically favoured particular methods and approaches.

The privileging of positivistic approaches, whereby knowledge can be scientifically verified through logical and/or mathematical proof, has become something of a gold standard in establishing 'knowledge'. The positivistic approach has proved persuasive within many professions, including early years, as it is deemed to provide a scientific rigour to the knowledge-base of the profession. For example, child development knowledge that draws on developmental psychology or neuroscience is seen to have a given rigour due to the methodological approaches adopted to establish it. Knowledge becomes that which can be validated via positivistic methods. There are other methods for determining knowledge, which will be tied to the traditions of different disciplines, but as will be explored in depth in Chapter 4, early years is multi-disciplinary, with different methods for determining and validating knowledge. This has arguably created a challenge for early years professionalism as the knowledge-base is potentially too disparate, but I think there are strengths to inter-disciplinarity.

It is important to recognise that the production and validation of knowledge frequently take place outside of the profession. The politicisation of professional knowledge is one component that has distorted the processes by which knowledge is determined and validated. As seen in Chapter 2, the political interest in quality early years services and professionalism has resulted in increased scrutiny of early years services, but also a desire for predictability. As policy makers set social welfare objectives for early years services, there is a desire to want to establish both what will support the meeting of those objectives and the tools to assess that the objectives have been met. The close tying of the professional role to the purpose of the profession implies technocratic models of professionalism in order to ensure the objectives of the profession are being met (Brock, 2013). Technocratic models of professionalism favour knowledge that can be observed and assessed (see Chapter 2) and are illustrative of the favouring of positivistic approaches in the validation of knowledge. The privileging of positivistic approaches is not solely about an epistemological hierarchy that has historically seen scientific rationality favoured as 'knowledge', it also imposes a top-down process in determining professional knowledge.

The top-down process is one whereby policy makers determine professional knowledge. Not only does this risk silencing knowledge from within the profession, but it can also restrict knowledge to that which can be assessed as 'effective' in meeting the political objectives (Campbell-Barr, 2018). Further, there is an implied assumption that there is a linear relationship between knowledge and the achievement of the desired outcomes (Brock, 2013; Urban et al., 2012). The determining and validating of professional knowledge are restricted by the objectives of policy.

Challenges to technocratic professionalism have sought to ask questions of the certainty of positivistic approaches to determining what is knowledge (in relation to both its identification and assessment) and to give voice to multiple perspectives on what knowledge is required for early years professionalism. Democratic approaches to determining a profession imply multiple ways of knowing and a willingness to examine personal and public assumptions of knowledge (Oberhuemer, 2005). The challenges to technocratic professionalism are as multi-disciplinary as the early years knowledge-base itself (Moss, 2017) and have been useful in considering processes of knowledge construction. However, challenges can also create uncertainty in what an early years professional is expected to know.

The questioning of knowledge can undermine knowledge and a personal sense of knowing. Questioning the construction of knowledge could imply there is no knowledge, only the power of the elite (those at the top of the hierarchy) to construct knowledge. Questions of the epistemological base can undermine the notion of science as truth, therefore raising further questions as to what is truth and how to determine something is 'true'. The questioning of knowledge and the processes by which the knowledge has been produced and evaluated all contribute to the potential uncertainty surrounding professional knowledge. There is a risk that the deconstruction of knowledge can result in deconstructing until there is nothing left (Young, 2007). However, it could be that the wrong questions are being asked as to what knowledge is.

In the next chapter I consider what constitutes the early years knowledge-base. What is important to determine here is that establishing what knowledge is will have different processes for determining and validating it, such as that tied to the disciplines or that which is associated with the politicisation of the purpose of the profession. Therefore, there is no single process for determining and validating what knowledge is. Just as the inter-disciplinarity of early years professionalism is an opportunity, so too are the variable ways of determining and validating knowledge. The different approaches to determining and validating knowledge give rise to knowledges, reflecting the rich and varied knowledge-base that supports early years professionals.

Knowledges and Skills

One of the challenges of tying knowledge to the purpose of the profession is that knowledge can be sidelined (Biesta, 2014). Technocratic models of professionalism are not concerned with knowledge, as knowledge alone will not produce the desired outcomes. Technocratic models of professionalism impose an emphasis on the application of knowledge. The focus on outcomes illustrates that there is a relationship between knowledge and its application in order for the outcome to be achieved. The application of knowledge is more than just a technique, which implies one way of doing things (such as a surgical technique): it is a skill, as it implies that the application of knowledge is contextually relevant (Winch, 2014). However, within technocratic models of professionalism (and the associated training of professionals) the contextual relevance reflects how professionals need to meet the demands of both policy and the labour market to ensure employability (see Chapter 2). There is an emphasis on professional competences to 'do' early years professionalism and to achieve the desired outcomes. The emphasis on the 'doing' (performing of competence) has arguably resulted in technocratic professionalism being more about technocratic skills, sidelining explorations of what knowledge is for early years professionalism.

Challenges to technocratic professionalism are not necessarily a rejection of positivistic approaches, nor of the importance of knowledge application, but a challenge to there being just one way of knowing, that knowledge can be certain and the notion of an end goal of 'knowing' that can be achieved. The challenges are important in highlighting that the relationship between knowledge and outcomes is far from linear, and there is certainly no easy formula of: Knowledge + Skills = Desired Outcomes.

Professional knowledge is actually about a complex relationship between knowledges and skills, in recognition that neither one alone constitutes professionalism. Knowledge alone does not enable a professional to meet the challenges of professional practice. Knowledge has to be combined with skill to enable the application of knowledges to meet the challenges of professional practice. Consider the training of early years professionals – the combination of knowledges and skills has parallels with the relationship between theory and practice (see Chapter 2), whereby a student is acquiring both theoretical and practical knowledges. In many ways it is like baking a cake – having the recipe, with the list of ingredients and instructions, does not mean an individual can bake a cake, it is the application that evidences the knowledges.

Skill implies being able to undertake tasks in contextually appropriate ways. Skills are not always describable, for example a skilled arts-person might not be able to provide a detailed description of their art. Professional knowledge is therefore about acquiring a set of knowledges that can support action, but as will be discussed, the knowledges take different forms and professional skill is not just a simple process of applying knowledge, but considering how to combine knowledges and how to evaluate knowledges.

Challenges to technocratic professionalism have been asking the wrong questions of professional knowledge. Rather than asking who constructs knowledge and what power inequalities are present within the knowledge construction, the questions should be about what the knowledges are for professionalism and how they are acquired and applied. Professional knowledge is therefore about a combination of identifying the knowledges that meet the needs of the profession (including knowledge acquaintances), considering how knowledge is acquired and its relationship to the practice of the profession.

━━━━━━━━━ **QUESTION** ━━━━━━━━━

Take a moment to consider the knowledges you think are needed to work in the early years. Consider which of the knowledges you would consider theoretical and those that could be regarded as everyday.

Knowledge Production

Sociological perspectives of professional knowledge help to illustrate my emphasis on knowledges and their relationship to skills. Sociological perspectives of knowledge recognise all knowledge as social, being relative to one's social position and socially constructed (Biesta, 2014) as well as derived from social experiences. As such, knowledge remains tied to the purpose of the profession and the role of the profession in meeting the needs of the social context. However, (as discussed) knowledge alone is not enough for professionalism as within professional contexts knowledge needs to be applied to meet the needs of the social context. Equally, however, it is not possible to have skill alone as this would silence knowledge. Therefore, there is a need to explore the relationships between knowledge and skill, and within sociological perspectives this entails considering how knowledge is determined, validated and applied, all of which are deeply social.

Bernstein was a British sociologist whose work focused on education, including thinking about professional knowledge within education (Bernstein, 1999, 2000). Bernstein built on the work of Durkheim in developing a sociology of knowledge, concerned with knowledge production and its different forms. Durkheim identified the origins of knowledge in religion, with esoteric knowledge and professionalism being located in a moral framework. Thus the early profession of priesthood (and even medicine) was shaped by technical activities within a spiritual, moral and ethical framework (Grace, 2014).

A cultural change from sacred (religious) societies to profane societies, where the hegemony of the church came to an end, gave rise to the professional principles of individualism, enterprise and reason (Young and Muller, 2014). The work of Durkheim is pertinent to the tensions identified within technocratic professionalism, where there is a focus on knowledge that can be observed and evidenced through positivistic approaches. However, identifying the origins of professional knowledge as within moral frameworks is important for beginning to appreciate that there are different forms of knowledge, with different processes of validation and application. Bernstein looked to further understand the conception of knowledge, including knowledge for professionals, as he was interested in the ways in which different forms of knowledge are realised (Hordern, 2017).

Bernstein's work, whilst important in providing a foundation for exploring professional knowledge and skills, is at times fragmented, and at others cryptic and even occasionally confusing. Fortunately, there are a number of others who have taken and developed the ideas of Bernstein (e.g. Hordern, 2017; Winch, 2014; Young and Muller, 2014) that I will draw upon in developing the discussion. Although I remain thankful to Bernstein for the development of my own knowledges on early years professionalism.

Bernstein (1999) distinguished between vertical and horizontal discourses, which enabled an exploration of how knowledge has different structures, but also the social conditions within which knowledge is produced, reproduced and validated. Vertical knowledge is explicit and structured, and can speak to other knowledge and history (Young and Muller, 2007). The strong structures of vertical knowledge enable it to be distributed and challenged, which can lead to shared conceptions (Hordern, 2016). Theoretical knowledge is a form of vertical discourse, with its value for a profession being in:

> The capacity of this knowledge to enable abstract conceptualisations, conjecture and hypothesis-building, taking the thinking beyond her immediate experience.
> (Hordern, 2017: 193)

The social validation of vertical discourse is evident in its support for the profession, because (as indicated by the quote above) it supports professionals in developing their professional thinking and practice. The sharing of the knowledge is a social process that enables it to be challenged and questioned, leading to shared (social) conceptions.

Embedded in the vertical discourse, Bernstein distinguishes between hierarchical knowledge structures and vertical knowledge structures. Given the potential confusion between vertical discourse and vertical knowledge structures, I will refer to vertical knowledge structures as 'segmented knowledge' (Hordern, 2017). Hierarchical knowledge is inward facing, creating a relatively coherent knowledge that can be tested and refuted through shared methodological and epistemological assumptions. The sciences offer an example of a vertical discourse with a hierarchical structure as the knowledge is identified as being robust, with agreed methodological processes with which to test the validity of the knowledge. Segmented knowledge structures have a range of different languages and/or perspectives, which form a discipline, but each with a different methodological and epistemological tradition, such as sociology and its various sub-disciplines. Whilst sociology is a recognised discipline, within it there are a number of different perspectives that have different methodological and epistemological traditions for testing and validating knowledge.

Whilst the distinction between hierarchical and segmented knowledge structures within vertical discourses might appear confusing, they are important for establishing that there are different forms of knowledge, with different structures and processes for testing and validating the knowledge. In simplistic terms, it illustrates that knowledge has varying structures and degrees of robustness to support its dissemination and analysis. Thus whilst some knowledge has a long history and is deemed robust, other forms of knowledge can be yet to establish their structure and validity. Consider, for example, the increasing influence of neuroscience in informing early years policy decisions (see Chapter 2), this can be attributed to its methodological foundations being grounded in the sciences, which I have already outlined are something of a gold standard for determining knowledge. If the process of validating neurosciences was not 'scientific' there would be a different epistemological base (both in regard to its structure and method for evaluation) to the knowledge, potentially weakening its perceived rigour and validity. Knowing the process by which knowledge has been produced and evaluated can give confidence (or not) in that knowledge.

Vertical discourse begins an appreciation for how early years professionalism requires knowledges of different forms and types. However, the inclusion of the horizontal discourse further enables professionals to recognise that knowledge is multiple and varied. The horizontal discourse represents local, context dependent, everyday and common sense knowledge. The knowledge is still social, whereby the local and everyday sharing of the knowledge will help ascribe meaning, such as knowing about the daily routine of an early years setting. Horizontal discourse therefore reflects knowledge that is based upon professional encounters. The process for validating horizontal knowledge is also embedded in the local, as it is the local context that both produces and validates the relevance of the knowledge. In recognising that early years professionalism requires knowledges, the combination of vertical discourse (with its different structures) and horizontal discourse provides a framework with which to appreciate the different ways of knowing for working with young children (see Table 3.1). Knowledge encompasses the theoretical (with varying degrees of robustness) and the everyday.

Table 3.1 Knowledge structures

Knowledge	Overview	Example
Vertical discourse	Explicit, structured	(see below)
Vertical discourse, hierarchical structure	Coherent, supporting dissemination and testing, the latter based on shared methodological and epistemological assumptions	Maths, sciences
Vertical discourse, segmented (horizontal) structure	Different languages and/or perspectives, with varying approaches for testing and validating	Sociology (and its sub-disciplines)
Horizontal discourse	Local, context dependent, everyday	Workplace specific knowledge

Adapted from Hordern (2017)

━━━━━━━━━━━ QUESTION ━━━━━━━━━━━

What do you think are the knowledges for early years professionalism? Consider both vertical (theoretical) and horizontal (everyday) knowledge and make a list of them.

Knowledge Application

Establishing that knowledge has different forms is important in valuing the rich and varied ways in which early years professionals know how to work with young children. However, knowledge alone will not be sufficient in ensuring professional practice. For example, an individual can read countless books on theories relating to child development, but this does not mean that they can then work with children. As already discussed, knowledge application is a key part of professionalism, but it is worth taking the time to consider how the process of knowledge application works.

As I have already stressed, knowledge application is not a simple linear process of taking knowledge X and applying it to achieve outcome Y. In fact, my emphasis on knowledges is about appreciating that early years professionalism will require a range of knowledges, both vertical and horizontal. In drawing on knowledges, the professional needs to know how to combine different knowledges and how to evaluate the success of the combinations. For example, returning to the idea of child development theories, these will combine with knowledge about the child, their family, the context of the early years setting, cultural understandings of early years provision, curriculum requirements, etc. to inform the early years professional. In the next chapter, I will outline in more detail the range of knowledges that an individual might draw upon in their professional practice, but here I want to further develop the sociological framework for considering how knowledges come together to inform professional practice.

Bernstein (2000) created a distinction between Singulars, Regions and Fields of Practice. A Singular can most easily be understood as a discipline: the academic, theoretical knowledge of the vertical discourse. Within Regions, different disciplines are brought together and recontextualised to inform the Field of Practice (Young and Muller, 2014). Regions enable professionals to draw on a range of knowledges and recontextualise them to meet the needs of real-life practice. The recontextualisation process is important, as this illustrates how knowledge is not taken in single or pure forms. Within Regions professionals bring together their specialised knowledge, including theories that have developed over time. Government, training providers, academics and professionals will all be involved in the process of recontextualising knowledge, whereby they draw upon disciplines to inform the provision of early years services. For example, as a lecturer in a university, I will draw upon different disciplines (Singulars) to inform the lectures that I deliver. However, in drawing on the disciplines I will be involved in a process of selecting, sequencing and pacing the disciplines. As such, I select particular parts of the early years knowledge-base and then order it and determine the way in which it is delivered to students. Students will then be involved in their own process of selecting, sequencing and pacing when using the knowledges to inform their professional practice. As such, all knowledge is taken to inform human activity *contextually*.

Early years professionalism is certainly multi-disciplinary (see Chapter 4), a Region that recontextualises the knowledge of different Singulars to inform the Field of Practice of working with young children. Fields of Practice therefore reflect the specialised, practical contexts of professionals.

Figure 3.1 (see next page) illustrates the relationships between Singulars, Regions and Fields of Practice. Importantly, the arrows face in two directions as Fields of Practice can give rise to new theories. As such, early years professionals can produce knowledge and, over time, through distribution and validation, this could give rise to new theories. Consider the early years pioneers in Chapter 1 – they were involved in generating new

Figure 3.1 Singulars, Regions and Fields of Practice

ideas about early years practice that over time have been shared and tested giving rise to their theoretical significance today.

The scribbles within Regions is to illustrate that drawing on knowledges to meet the needs of professional practice is a messy process and highlights that the relationships between Singulars, Regions and Fields of Practice are not as neat and linear as the arrows might imply. The messiness symbolises the messiness of professional practice. Therefore, it is not sufficient to appreciate that early years professionalism requires knowledges. Knowing only comes after action, with a requirement to both know how to evaluate knowledge and how to evaluate knowledge combinations.

Early years professionals need to understand the reach, power and usefulness of different forms of knowledge and how they can negotiate their way around them. In part, this will relate back to the processes for validating knowledge and being able to determine between good and bad reason. The evaluation of knowledge is also tied to knowledge combinations and considering where knowledges complement or contradict each other. The evaluation of knowledges will be based on factors such as epistemological hierarchies that favour positivism, the history of the knowledge (longevity often supports credibility), but also personal epistemological perspectives as to what forms sound reason. As such, an early years professional who is reading any academic article (for example) will evaluate it based on its theoretical position, methods, who wrote it, etc.

Early years professionals therefore need to know which forms of knowledge are non-negotiable and which are discretional. Non-negotiable knowledge may not be vertical discourse, with its structure, as all workplaces will have habits and assumptions that form the basis of professional practice. In many respects, the process of evaluating knowledges (and their varying combinations) will be in relation to their usefulness – has the knowledge met the needs of professional practice?

The meeting of the needs of professional practice might be relatively straightforward in some professions where there are agreed processes and procedures for undertaking particular tasks. For early years professionalism, the very nature of working with young children means that there is very little that is straightforward. Knowledge combinations will vary between children, but the success of the knowledge combinations can also change with time. The changes with time are not just in relation to how working with a two year old may vary to working with a four year old (i.e. the child has changed with time), but also that even on a daily basis, what worked in meeting the needs of an upset child on one day might require a different set of actions to meet their needs on a different day. As such, the process of coming to 'know' is continuous and ongoing.

The ongoing process of coming to know how to be an early years professional illustrates that practice is central to professionalism. Whilst I have emphasised that knowledge has to be applied to be professional knowledge, it is also that the experiential learning of being in practice will also contribute to the process of coming to know how to work with young children. Experience provides the 'doing' (applying of knowledge) in context, with professional training providing the opportunity to acquire knowledge for action. All knowledge is therefore social, both in regard to how the social context will determine the relevance of knowledge and how the social will be involved in the evaluation of knowledge and its distribution. Knowledge is not 'out there', disembodied from early years professionals, but grounded in the social interactions of the profession.

Conclusion

Knowledge has been much debated, theorised and questioned over time, but what I am keen to stress is that knowledge comes in different shapes and sizes. My emphasis on the variability of knowledges is to provide a framework for considering the rich and varied ways in which early years professionals come to know. As outlined in Chapter 1, there has been a historical devaluing of working with young children, alongside a construction of working with young children as merely requiring natural ability. However, I want to draw attention to, and celebrate, just how complex coming to know how to be an early years professional is.

Sociological perspectives of knowledge provide a model with which professionals can draw upon a range of knowledges to inform their professional practice. The focus on knowledges provides many prospects, through facilitating the opportunities that an inter-disciplinary knowledge-base offers, whilst drawing on both theoretical and everyday knowledge. For me, sociological perspectives enable an appreciation of just how much early years professionals know.

CHAPTER SUMMARY

- Knowledge is multiple and varied, with different structures and processes for sharing and validating it.
- Early years professionalism requires knowledges, both theoretical (vertical) and everyday (horizontal).
- Knowledge alone is not enough for professionalism. Knowing only comes after action.
- Knowledge will be evaluated in relation to how different forms of knowledge come together to meet the needs of practice.
- Coming to know is a continuous and ongoing process.
- Early years professionals know in rich and varied ways.

FURTHER READING

Hordern, J. (2016). 'Knowledge, practice, and the shaping of early childhood professionalism', *European Early Childhood Education Research Journal*, 24(4), 508–20.

This is a useful article for further exploring the work of Bernstein in relation to early years professionalism.

Nursery World Jobs Board: https://www.nurseryworldjobs.co.uk/

Nursery World is a practitioner magazine based in the UK. Have a look at their jobs board and consider the kinds of knowledge and skills that are being asked for. What is it that early years professionals are expected to know?

4

THE EARLY YEARS KNOWLEDGE-BASE

In this chapter I explore the early years professional knowledge-base. As I have set out in the previous chapter, I see knowledge for professionalism as plural, with knowledges that have different structures and processes for evaluating it. I also see professional knowledge as an ongoing process of continual professional learning rather than an end goal that can be reached. Further, I recognise that professional knowledge only comes from the process of applying knowledge in practice. Therefore, my intention in this chapter is to explore knowledges and skills very broadly, in order to begin to consider what constitutes the early years knowledge-base. The items discussed and presented are not intended as a checklist, but as a discussion of the plurality of knowledges and skills. Throughout the chapter I encourage readers to consider how the different knowledges and skills come together and how the combinations vary in order to meet the needs of the context. Therefore, what is presented in this chapter is not an exhaustive list of knowledges and skills, but the beginnings of a process of recognising and celebrating the rich and varied ways that early years professionals know how to work with young children.

A Multi-disciplinary Knowledge-base

The early years is a multi-disciplinary profession. The multi-disciplinarity reflects that knowledge has different structures, encompassing vertical discourse and its hierarchical and segmented structures (see Chapter 3). Within the vertical discourse, there is a range of disciplines that underpin early years professionalism. As Rhedding-Jones (2005) notes, the early years is something of a theoretical hybrid, with its roots in developmental psychology being joined by socio-cultural theories and more recently sociology. Within these broad theoretical perspectives there will be a range of sub-disciplines. For example, developmental psychology is a broad field with a range of perspectives, that have been very influential in the early years (Vincent and Braun, 2011). Equally, Chapter 3 has already illustrated how sociology is a broad discipline, with many different perspectives, with the sociology of childhood growing in prominence and influence within the early years. The different disciplines that inform early years professionalism reflect the vertical discourse, with a segmented (horizontal) structure, as outlined in Chapter 3, whereby the varying sub-disciplines have a range of languages, perspectives and processes for validating and testing knowledge.

Internationally, the theoretical hybridity of early years professionalism is recognised. For example, Li and Chen (2016) discuss how psychology, philosophy and sociology are the theoretical foundations of the early years in China, whilst in Hungary pedagogue students study subjects in psychology and the social sciences (Oberhuemer et al., 2010). However, beyond the disciplinary cores of early years professionalism, it is also possible to see the practical aspects of professionalism having an influence. For example, Hungarian students also learn about curriculum methodology, whilst in Croatia, students will undertake subjects in pedagogy, general psychology, psychology of education, didactics (a theory of teaching that emphasises the practical aspects) and methodology (Dubovicki and Jukić, 2017).

Other influences within early years professionalism include curriculum studies, social policy, health, cultural studies and family studies (Brock, 2013; Dalli, 2008). However, it is worth pausing to consider that the degree to which each of these subjects influences the early years knowledge-base will be culturally specific. For example, the disciplinary core might be more weighted towards developmental psychology than sociology as the result of local evolutions in research, subject development and localised perspectives on what constitutes 'valid' knowledge. Equally, the cultural context can give rise to a focus on particular topics. For example within England, the political interest in early years services and professionals means that social policy and politics increasingly feature in higher (degree level) training. Whilst in Hungary students will undertake subjects in Hungarian culture, art and music, reflecting a nationalistic education model that has emerged following the fall of Communism (Campbell-Barr, 2017a). The examples of England and Hungary demonstrate that the influences on the early years knowledge-base are far ranging, but also contextually specific.

The multi-disciplinarity of early years professionalism means that those studying to work with young children will be undertaking a range of subjects. There is no simple process of studying an early years-ology. The range of theoretical perspectives encompassed within the early years knowledge-base begins to illustrate some of the challenges of learning to work with young children. However, it is also important to recognise that often theories have been critiqued and challenged and that there can be different perspectives from within theories. For example, the historical influence of developmental psychology in early years professionalism has been challenged by socio-cultural perspectives (Krieg, 2010). Post-structural perspectives have questioned both the epistemological base of developmental theories and the hierarchies of power in the production of knowledge. Therefore, whilst developmental psychology is recognised as a theoretical core for early years professionalism, there is no one interpretation of it. Further, there are challenges to the different interpretations of developmental psychology that do exist, creating potential instability in the early years knowledge-base.

The disciplines that inform early years professionalism are not necessarily in harmony with one another, but this is reflective of how there are different perspectives on the role of early years services. The latter is particularly important when taking into consideration the views of different stakeholders. Whilst policy makers, early years professionals and parents might all be interested in child development, this does not equate to them interpreting it in the same way.

The recognition that there are different perspectives within academic disciplines, as well as varying interpretations amongst stakeholders of early years services and early years professionals, illustrates that the early years knowledge-base is not a fixed entity. As illustrated in Chapter 1, early years professionals are the meeting place for different perspectives on early years services and the associated disciplines that underpin them. Being an early years professional is therefore not about establishing a fixed knowledge-base, but about recognising what are the core constituents of the knowledge-base and beginning to consider how they might come together – the knowledge combinations – to inform professional practice.

However, rather than providing an unstable foundation on which to explore early years professionalism, I think that the fluidity of the knowledge-base and the challenges within and between disciplines provide opportunities. Importantly, the fluidity of the knowledge-base enables professional practice to keep evolving and for new theories to emerge. Early years professionalism will not stagnate in one particular model of child development, but will be able to draw upon the range of perspectives to develop, evolve and experiment with professional practice. In particular, as outlined in Chapter 3, it could be that it is early years professionals who will give rise to the next theories for the early years professional knowledge-base.

The multi-disciplinarity of early years professionalism therefore acts as a strength for the profession. The strength comes from the willingness to consider different perspectives and being open to challenge, as this can give rise to new ideas and theories.

However, the challenge for early years professionals is that there is a lot that they are expected to know, with clear questions as to what degree of depth an individual needs to understand the range of disciplines.

Whilst I see there being strength in the multi-disciplinarity of early years professionalism, I am also aware that it does create a challenge for the profession. Not having a single disciplinary core, with agreed methods for evaluating and validating knowledge, weakens the structure of the knowledge-base. Inevitably, this perceived weakness is based upon a favouring of positivistic knowledge traditions (see Chapter 3). However, for those outside of the profession, the weak structure of the knowledge-base could equate to a weak profession. Articulating the early years professional knowledge-base is therefore part of a process of demonstrating the full range of knowledges for working with young children and the complexities of being an early years professional.

Knowledge

As has been demonstrated in Chapter 3, knowledge is multiple and varied in how it is structured, distributed and validated, spanning from the theoretical to the everyday. The CoRe project (Urban et al., 2011) that explored competence requirements for early years professionals in Europe has been useful in providing a starting point for considering the knowledges required of the early years workforce. In the review Urban et al. identified the following forms of knowledge:

> ... knowledge of children's development and learning; knowledge of didactics and teaching methods; knowledge of different teaching subjects; knowledge of children's rights; knowledge of the ECEC [early childhood education and care] system and regulations; knowledge of children's hygiene, health, nutrition and safety. (Urban et al., 2011: 55)

The quote is illustrative of the discussion presented so far and how early years professionals draw on theories of child development and pedagogical practice in culturally relevant ways. For example, knowledge of systems and regulations, including those of health and hygiene, reflects that theories on child development are not just applied to shape pedagogical practice, but that the application will be in relation to the confines of local early years requirements. Early years professionals therefore combine their knowledge of child development with knowledge about any local curriculum or other regulatory requirements. As seen earlier in the chapter, the combinations of knowledges may not always be harmonious. At times regulatory requirements might impose a particular reading onto child development, such as early years services being concentrated on the social welfare function of narrowing the gap in the educational performance of children from different socio-economic groups (see Chapter 2). Equally, curriculum requirements may not seem in harmony with knowledge of the didactics and teaching methods most appropriate for the early years (for example). Knowledge combinations are therefore complex, illustrating the importance of evaluating the combinations, possibly giving rise to alternative combinations.

━━━━━━━━━━ QUESTION ━━━━━━━━━━

Consider your own early years context and the regulatory requirements that exist. How do the regulatory requirements complement and/or conflict with your child development knowledge?

Understanding knowledge combinations is important for recognising where knowledges complement each other and where they conflict. The combinations of different forms of knowledge illustrate that those working in the early years need to know how to apply knowledge and how to evaluate it (Winch, 2014). Whilst complementing knowledge combinations can facilitate professional practice, being aware of the conflicting knowledge combinations is also significant for developing a personal understanding of the knowledges that are important for early years professionalism. The combinations of knowledges can further contribute to the contestable nature of knowledge as the context rarely demands the same knowledge combinations. Being aware of knowledge conflicts and contestability can facilitate a process of considering different knowledge combinations, or, in the case of regulatory requirements, mediating knowledges to inform pedagogical practice. Knowledge is not certain, but temporal, whereby it is specific to the context (Biesta, 2014). The notion of knowledge as truth might not reflect an individual's perception of truth, but the combination of knowledges that meet the demands of the context at a given time.

The focus on a given time is important as early years is a challenging context that shifts and adapts over the course of a day, week, month and year. For example, the knowledges required at the start of a new academic year may reflect those related to supporting children's transitions, whilst at another point they might be about identifying children with additional needs. The stating of 'knowing' is far from fixed.

Pedagogical knowledge

Pedagogical knowledge represents a key meeting point between knowledge and its application for early years professionals. Pedagogical knowledge is about the construction of the learning environment, both in regard to the provision of resources and how adults will interact with children to support their development (Moloney, 2010b). The support for child development already illustrates how pedagogical knowledge will be derived from knowledge combinations. Embedded in pedagogical knowledge is an understanding of the child and their ability, knowledge of how children learn and child development, as well as knowledge of the environment and resources and how they can facilitate children's learning.

Knowledge of how children learn in the early years is influenced by a construction of a child as a competent learner. The influence of romantic concepts of childhood and early years pioneers such as Pestalozzi, Froebel and the McMillan sisters (see Chapter 1) has helped to contribute to a view of the child as an active, independent learner, who learns 'best when they are actively involved in negotiating their own learning and exploring their own interests' (MacFarlane and Lewis, 2012: 68-67). Formal, teacher led approaches to early years education are often identified as misplaced, as the child is positioned as passive within the learning environment. Instead, the child as a competent learner comes to the learning environment with their own knowledge and interests, which the early years professional seeks to foster.

Child-centred has come to epitomise early years pedagogical knowledge as the focus is on the child at the centre of their learning as opposed to the focus being on the professional directing the child's learning. Kuisma and Sandberg (2008) discuss those undertaking early years training in Sweden, and the role of the preschool teacher in skilfully responding to children, through developing activities that have the child and their interests at the centre. Moloney (2010b) identifies child-centred pedagogy as a part of Irish policy rhetoric, but also raises questions as to what this means in practice. Thus the skilful responding of the teacher is a subtle and not always overt application of knowledge. However, whilst it is possible to identify child-centred as being complex, the complexity is compounded by it being a term that is variably interpreted. Historical influences, along with cultural interpretations, mean that child-centred is a multifaceted term.

Broadly, child-centred has three core ideas of romanticism, developmentalism and equality (Campbell-Barr, 2017a). The three interpretations are not mutually exclusive, but illustrate the historical influence of romantic concepts of children as naturally curious, the dominance of developmental psychology within the early years and more recent egalitarian perspectives, motivated by an increased awareness of children's rights.

The varying perspectives on child-centred pedagogy illustrate the conflicts that can arise between the knowledges for early years professionalism. On the one hand, interpretations of child-centred approaches offer the opportunity to recognise children's autonomy, whilst, on the other, being shaped by prescriptive perspectives of children's development (Walkerdine, 1984). The dominance of developmental theories within the early years knowledge-base is arguably underpinned by a desire to demonstrate the effectiveness of romantic constructs of children as competent, capable and independent learners. The interest in being able to demonstrate the effectiveness of early years services, along with the favouring of positivistic approaches (see Chapter 3) to demonstrate that early years services 'work' created something of a paradox between a liberatory, romantic pedagogy and evidence of developmental effectiveness (Walkerdine, 1984). The use of child-centred therefore illustrates the theoretical hybridity of the early years and the potential for conflicting ideas that early years professionals are required to negotiate.

Further challenges are evident within interpretations of child-centredness when considering that it is *a child* that is being centred, when in reality early years professionals work with groups of children. How can all children be autonomous and pursue their own interests in support of their individual development when there is a group of

20 children? The combination of knowledges is really emphasised when considering how professionals meet the needs and interests of a group of children. As such, the pedagogical knowledge of being child-centred is not only about knowing each child within the group, but also about knowing how to meet the needs of the group.

QUESTION

Consider the terms child-centred and children-centred – which one do you think you try to adopt as a professional and why?

Frequently, play-based approaches are referred to as being both pedagogically appropriate in the early years and in support of children-centred approaches. The emphasis on play is evident within early years curriculums such as the Early Years Foundation Stage in England and Aistear in Ireland, although reference to play in a curriculum document cannot predict what this will look like in practice or whether the interpretations of play in the curriculum are the same as those of other stakeholders. Just as child-centred can be variously interpreted, so can the use of 'play-based'. In a recent research project that I undertook with colleagues in Croatia, Denmark, England, Ireland, Italy and Spain (Campbell-Barr et al., 2018) exploring interpretations of child-centredness, our examples from practice illustrated that 'play' was one of the core categories for understanding child-centredness, but that it encompassed heuristic play, physical play, symbolic play, pretence/socio-dramatic play and play with rules, when considering the kind of play activities. However, in addition there was also the role of the child(ren) in the play, such as solitary (independent) play, onlooker play, parallel play, associative play and cooperative play.

Despite recognition for the different forms of play, Wood (2008) has discussed that play could favour some children over others. Embedded in the different forms of play is a construction of the child who not only knows how to play, but also knows the rules of the play. The focus on the 'competent' child could risk overstating and/or over-claiming a child's competence, whereby the assumption of competence results in limiting the child's participation. In an observation undertaken in Denmark, there was an example of an early years professional supporting a child to participate in a game of chase (Campbell-Barr et al., 2018). The child was new to the group and therefore did not know the rules of the chase game. The professional excitedly encouraged the new child's participation, before allowing the child to enjoy the chase game on their own. However, if the professional had assumed the child had the competence to play chase, the child would have risked being marginalised from the game. Therefore, whilst play is often seen to be child-centred and offering equality of participation, it might not be for all children (Wood, 2008). The example illustrates the role of the professional and their knowledges in facilitating the child's play.

The various ways to refer to play demonstrate that it is easy to get caught up in the analysis of terms and to debate their meaning, which (as I have outlined) can result in uncertainty as to what terms mean. Instead, I think it is important to recognise the challenges of what early years professionals are expected to know. My own students often express their frustration at a common perception that working with children means you just play all day, but in exploring pedagogical knowledge alone as a part of the early years knowledge-base, it is possible to highlight that the knowledge-base is underpinned by multiple theoretical perspectives, with equally variable conceptions and realities. Pedagogical knowledge is hugely complex, drawing on a range of knowledges to inform professional skills.

Everyday knowledge

Everyday knowledge represents the segmented (horizontal) knowledge for early years professionalism that is not based in theory, philosophy or regulatory knowledge, but is nonetheless an important part of the early years professional knowledge-base. Everyday knowledge is hard to define and articulate, because (as discussed in Chapter 3) it is tied to the context, being local and embedded in the everyday. The difficulty with segmented knowledge is that it is not always written down, fully articulated or tangible. Segmented knowledge is therefore often devalued (if valued at all), because it is not always evident; instead it is taken for granted. The devaluing of segmented knowledge is based within epistemological hierarchies that favour knowledge that can be seen, observed and evaluated, but within early years professionalism everyday knowledge is important.

Everyday knowledge is often practically orientated, being both pertinent to day-to-day practice and being derived from practice. Payler and Locke (2013) explore how early years professionals in England favour knowledge that is viewed as practical rather than theoretical as it feels more relevant for day-to-day practice. Theoretical knowledge can feel abstract and dislocated from both practice and the individual as they have little power or control over it (Bernstein, 2000). The practicality of everyday knowledge means it is lived by experienced professionals, which supports its relevance. However, everyday knowledge is not an excuse to ignore theory. Theory does hold relevance for practice, as it is the combination of theory with everyday knowledge that meets the needs of the context. As such, the process of recontextualising Singulars (theory) within Regions is about meeting the needs of the Field of Practice (see Chapter 3). Professional knowledge is both that which stems from theory and that which comes from the everyday.

There are parallels in considering the ways in which children learn and how knowledge is established and acquired for early years professionals. The notion of the competent child, who comes with their own knowledge when they enter an early years centre, equally relates to a view of a competent professional who comes with *their* own knowledge (see Chapters 5 and 7). As such, some of the everyday knowledge that practitioners have acquired will have come from experiences of caring for and looking after younger family members, such as siblings or one's own children. Other forms of daily knowledge will come from experiences of working with children within early years settings, such as learning about the daily routine of a setting and how particular routines and activities are undertaken (see Chapter 7). Knowledge about the day-to-day running of an early years centre provides important workplace knowledge.

Workplace knowledge (and other forms of everyday knowledge) come from a process of 'classifying phenomena according to similar features' (Guile, 2014: Loc2088). Social scientific concepts can become a resource that is embedded in social practices, such as the ways in which a curriculum is delivered in an early years setting. Normative ways of acting evolve, where there is not necessarily a given logic to the actions, but there is a degree of justification that implies logic. For example, imagine starting a new job in a nursery, where after lunch the staff begin to lay out beds in one of the rooms so that the children can have a sleep. The beds are laid out in a particular pattern, there is no logic to the pattern, it is just the way the beds have always been laid out. Whilst this example offers a very practical one, the same can be said of other aspects of early years practice, such as play-based approaches being advocated and adopted, because that is what has always happened.

Workplace knowledge encompasses socially accepted ways of being and working with children. As I explore in subsequent chapters, there are some commonalities in the socially accepted ways of working with children that have evolved over time. However, there can also be cultural variations. The variations are what can stimulate perceptions of something being strange or different when visiting an early years setting in another country, but for the professionals working there it is a part of their workplace knowledge. Workplace knowledge is not solely constructed in the workplace, but also as a response to the wider social context. Workplace knowledge is therefore an important part of everyday knowledge and supports being an early years professional.

Chapter 7 will explore everyday knowledge in more depth, but what is important to emphasise here is both that knowledge has different forms and structures, and that the knowledges that professionals generate from the everyday (horizontal discourse) are just as important as theoretical knowledge (vertical discourse). However, the challenge of the everyday is that it is not easily transferable. Therefore, the everyday knowledge that meets the needs of the context in a nursery in Plymouth in the UK will be different to that of the knowledges required in a preschool in Portogruaro, Italy. Thus knowledge is always developing and evolving.

Skills

Knowledge can be regarded as 'out there', often feeling intangible and irrelevant until it is put into action. The application of knowledge is central to professionalism, but the application requires the practising of knowledges in contextually relevant ways. The process of learning to become an early years professional is about the acquisition of knowledges for the purpose of action. However, knowledges only become real and relevant after the action. For example, the preference for experiential knowledge reflects that the action (the professional practice) has helped to meet the needs of the context. Learning knowledges is about mastering how the knowledges are represented – what they look like in practice. Transferring knowledge into practice is about how knowledges participate in practice. Professionals therefore need to know how to combine knowledges, how to apply the knowledge combinations and how to evaluate them, particularly in relation to how the knowledges have met the needs of the context (Winch, 2014). Knowledge and skills are therefore deeply entwined.

Within Anglo-Saxon countries, often the focus on knowing-how is reduced to skill, but it is important to emphasise that to have skill is to acquire the ability to undertake tasks in contextually relevant conditions (Winch, 2014). As explored in earlier chapters, the conditions can be constraining and demanding, so the early years professional and their personal characteristics will be involved in the process of combining, evaluating and applying knowledges. Skill should not be oversimplified. There are many skills that are referred to within professional contexts, such as people skills, time management skills and planning skills, that make them appear ubiquitous. However, in considering planning skills it is possible to identify that an individual can exercise planning skills without actually planning. As such they can go through the motions of making a plan, but without considering what the outcomes of the plan will be in relation to the context (Winch, 2014). Professional skills are therefore far more complex than they might first appear.

Skills are not as simple as the skill of child development or didactics in combination with knowledge about the children one works with and workplace knowledge. Instead, the skills of creating the pedagogic environment, alongside forming relationships with children, encompass the knowledges that have been discussed above, but with no simple linear relationships between knowledges and skills, or no obvious ways in which to combine knowledges. In addition, Chapter 7 will discuss the skill of reflective practice as this is central in understanding the entwining of knowledges and skills, but here I will consider the skills of pedagogical environments and relationships.

Creating pedagogical environments

The creation of the pedagogic environment relates to early years professionals considering how they structure the environment and the resources they will introduce to that environment (Moloney, 2010b), alongside the role that they undertake in support of children's development. The resources will reflect the ages of the children and their interests, encompassing developmental knowledge and knowledge of the children.

The role of the early years professional within that environment will be multiple and varied. For example, it might be that of playing alongside the children, initiating play, facilitating play or directing play and learning (Campbell-Barr et al., 2018). In the cross-European project exploring child-centred practice, I worked with colleagues to explore the ways in which professionals move from being alongside, within and away from the activities that children were undertaking, but also how a professional can undertake multiple positions at any one time (Campbell-Barr et al., 2018). For example, a professional may be within a game of chase, whilst also being alongside (and thus supporting) another group of children in a mud kitchen. Professionals skilfully adjust their role within the pedagogic environment in support of children's different forms of play.

Professionals also use other skills, such as exposing children to language to support language development (Jensen et al., 2010). For example, professionals will narrate activities or repeat the words of children in order to expose them to vocabulary. However, there will also be more subtle, perhaps non-describable skills that professionals will be enacting. For example, in Denmark, Jensen (2015) reviewed the skills of early years professionals in creating pedagogic environments that reveal the child as competent and capable in support of democratic spaces. The focus on democratic spaces reflects a particular knowledge construction of the child: the democratic view of child-centredness. The early years professional will pace and sequence activities, provide resources and engage with children in support of the democratic view of the child, facilitating choice and active participation. The creation of the pedagogic environment is therefore a complex set of skills that draws upon a range of knowledges, but also illustrates that there is not just one way of creating a pedagogic environment.

Forming relationships

The role of the early years professional in supporting the democratic view of the child illustrates that an early years professional is doing more than just establishing the pedagogic environment. The role of the professional within the environment illustrates how the pedagogic environment is more than just the structural. Early years professionals need to know and form relationships with the children that they work with to support the construction of the pedagogic environment. Early years professionals therefore form relationships with children in multiple ways to support the pedagogic environment, such as anticipating and responding to the emotions of the children in support of building excitement and/or interest or providing comfort and familiarity (Campbell-Barr et al., 2018).

The interpersonal aspect of early years professionalism is well documented in relation to attachment theory. Attachment theory stems from developmental psychology and states the importance of children forming attachments with significant adults in support of the children's personal development (Holmes, 2012). The attachment provides a sense of security, from which children can broaden their development. Attachment theory is a wide-ranging field and illustrative of the contestable and changing nature of knowledge within the early years. Rather than repeating the well-documented debates on attachment theory, my interest is in the emphasis placed on professionals to form relationships with children. Considering attachments under skills highlights how early years professionals are expected to apply knowledge in order to form relationships with children. The forming of relationships is not simple, often with little specification about what the attachments should look like in practical terms (Page and Elfer, 2013). There is much that can disturb and disrupt the attachment between the professional and a child, demonstrating that attachments are an ongoing skill for the early years professional rather than a fixed goal to be reached.

From my own work researching how pedagogue students in Hungary form loving relations with the children they work with (Campbell-Barr, 2017a), I am aware that those training to work with young children are conscious of the importance of forming relationships with children, but that knowing *how* to form the relationships is much harder. Students were very aware of the cultural ideal of being a loving pedagogue, but were less certain about what this looked like in practice, particularly when the children may have been tentative or shy in approaching them. Students would be advised on providing hugs and ensuring they said hello to children on their arrival at the kindergarten, but the simplistic guidance on enactments of love did not reflect the depth of understanding of the cultural ideal of the loving pedagogue. As such, students could exercise the skill of forming relationships with children, but this did not mean that the relationships had formed, and they were acutely aware of this difference.

The emphasis on being a loving pedagogue in Hungary gives precedence to a particular reading of the emotional relationship between the professional and the child, but it is equally important that the relationship between the adult and the children can support a range of emotions such as anticipation and excitement, as well as happiness and joy and frustration and anger. The latter illustrate that the supporting of emotions can be challenging and that working with children cannot be assumed to be all hugs and smiles (see Chapter 6). Forming relationships with children is not an easy skill to acquire and illustrates how knowing that you need to form relationships is very different from knowing how to enact and foster those relationships.

The relationships that early years professionals have to form extend beyond the relationships with children to encompass relationships with colleagues and parents. Lazzari (2012), writing about Bologna in Italy, discusses how relationships between colleagues have become a deeply entwined aspect of early years professionalism. However, the relationships are inevitably shaped by the local context and regulations, such as adult to child ratios and whether there is a nominated leader or manager that imposes some degree of relational hierarchy. For example, relationships with colleagues will be very different for a childminder, providing early years services within their own home, to that of a manager of a large group of day nurseries. Theories of leadership have been well documented, including the different ways in which workplace relationships can be structured and enacted within early years environments, from more hierarchical ones to those grounded on principles of equality and collaboration (see Campbell-Barr and Leeson, 2016, for further discussion), but here I want to focus on the relationships with parents.

Relationships between early years professionals and parents are increasingly recognised internationally as important to the overall quality of early years services (European Commission, 2014; OECD, 2011). Strong relationships are seen to support better learning outcomes and academic success for children, particularly those from disadvantaged backgrounds. Despite the recognition for strong relationships between professionals and parents, there is little certainty as to what these relationships look like and how they are enacted.

The relationships between professionals and parents will be subject to the context in which they are located. For example, market orientated early years models position parents as consumers of a service, often involving a monetary transaction. However, the service is one that concerns the care and education of a child. The monetary transaction is therefore very different from that of buying a car or a loaf of bread, as the relationship between the professional and parent becomes caught up in understanding what the relationship between the professional and the child will look like.

The relationship between the professional and the child will be shaped by the expectations of the parents, irrespective of if they are paying for the service. Parents can demand explicit enactments of professional–child relationships (Van Laere et al., 2018), such as providing a cuddle after a child falls over or for the professional to physically interact with the child or to bathe the child in language. The enactments will be variable between parents and also subject to culturally appropriate responses (see Chapter 1). Relationships with parents therefore demand that the professional is able to read parents and adjust to them, such as knowing how to talk to them appropriately (Ward, 2018). However, the early years professional is not just reading how to form a relationship with a parent, but also reading what that parent expects of the relationship between the professional and the child. The relationship can therefore be regarded as one that has different layers.

The forming of relationships with parents is a recognised challenge for early years professionals, with there often being little exploration of parental relationships within initial training and students even shrinking away from recognition of the importance of these relationships (Visković and Višnjić Jevtić, 2017; Ward, 2018). From my own work with students, I know that there can be struggles of being positioned as 'the student' – an apprentice who is still a novice within the profession. Yet the novice label contrasts with the knowledges that the student is acquiring and that, at times, a student might want to share those knowledges, but is unsure of how to form the relationship in order to do so.

There appears to be a preference to refer to 'parental partnership' to illustrate a non-hierarchical relationship between the professional and the parent, but hierarchies are present. Hierarchies can emerge as a result of the context, whereby parents may prefer to communicate with more senior members of staff. Further, despite the egalitarian driven use of the term partnership, the emphasis appears to be on the role of the professional in forming the partnership, but with clear expectations regarding parents. Parents are assumed to have the necessary **cultural capital** to feel confident to engage with professionals (Van Laere et al., 2018) and to know how the partnership will operate.

Cultural capital represents the social assets that an individual has, which they can then draw upon to gain an advantage in life. Cultural capital encompasses the objectified (objects such as books and pictures that symbolise wealth), the institutionalised (the school or university a person attended) and the embodied (lasting dispositions of the mind) (Bourdieu, 2008). Whilst an individual might be able to acquire objects and attend institutions that symbolise wealth, the embodied state represents that there are particular ways of thinking amongst social groups that might not be shared between groups. Within parental partnerships, cultural capital refers to the assumption that parents have the necessary dispositions of the mind (the knowledge of what a partnership is and the skill to enact it) to be able to comfortably engage in the partnership. However, if I liken parental partnerships to when I take my motorbike to the garage, I do not have the knowledge and skills to be able to fully understand what the mechanic is telling me is wrong with my motorbike – I do not have the necessary capital and thus I feel marginalised from the exchange of ideas. Even for parents that might have the necessary cultural capital and an understanding of what the partnership will look like, there is still an assumption that they have the time to work in partnership with professionals.

There appears to be something of a continual paradox whereby professionals know about the importance of working in partnership with parents, but can find it hard to form relationships, due to both practical issues, such as parents having the time, and challenges of knowing what the knowledge looks like in practice. And yet, despite parents also wanting to form relationships with professionals and to know more about what their children have been up to, they can fear wasting the professional's time or not feel confident enough to engage with the professional. The paradox is a clear illustration of the tension between knowing about parental partnerships and enacting it.

Know-that and Know-how

The example of parental partnerships illustrates that professionalism is more than just knowledges as there is a requirement to enact the knowledges. However, throughout the chapter it has been evident that the enactment of knowledges is not a simple relationship between a single knowledge becoming a skill. My emphasis on knowledges and skills in the plural has been about appreciating the complexities of the early years professional knowledge-base. Not only is there no single form of knowledge to inform early years professional practice, the knowledges will be multiple and varied for all early years professionals in relation to the context. The enactment of knowledge will therefore vary as a result of the knowledge combinations, such as knowing about the importance of parental partnerships, but also knowing that a parent works or lacks the confidence to come to the early years setting. Being an early years professional is both a highly knowledgeable and skilled profession.

Winch (2010, 2014) writes of a distinction between know-that and know-how. Know-that refers to expertise, theory and propositions (statements of judgement or hypotheses), but by itself know-that cannot constitute professional knowledge. A professional needs know-how to apply knowledge. The application of knowledge is skilled, as know-how is more than just a describable procedure, as this would depict a technical application. Rather, know-how requires the application of knowledge in relation to the context. The context requires that the professional not only knows how to apply the knowledge, but also that they understand the reach and the power of that knowledge. Professionals also need to know which knowledge is negotiable and how they are able to negotiate it. In negotiating the different knowledges to inform professional practice, the professional also needs to know how to combine different forms of knowledge and how to evaluate them (see Chapter 7).

Early years professionals are involved in a process of continually exploring knowledge combinations: drawing on multiple theoretical perspectives in combination with pedagogic, everyday and workplace knowledge to inform their daily interactions with children. Professionals will shift and adjust their knowledge combinations in order to respond to the needs of different children (and parents), thus enacting multiple knowledge combinations at any one time. Exploring the early years knowledge-base enables a consideration of the knowledgeable and skilled work of early years professionals.

Conclusion

My exploration of knowledge and skills within this chapter is not exhaustive. There is much that I have not discussed, such as how knowledge is political, framed by debates on race and class. For example, I have not considered knowledge around inclusion and how this might be enacted to represent a skilled professional. However, my intention has always been to begin a process of bringing knowledges back into early years professionalism.

I am continually amazed by the careful, skilled and knowledgeable work of early years professionals. Whilst the range of knowledges that inform the early years professional knowledge-base can be confusing for professionals as they seek to negotiate their way between them, and there is the challenge that a lack of a clear disciplinary core weakens the structure of the knowledge-base, I maintain my position of amazement. My amazement is in observing early years professionals as they adjust their knowledge combinations to meet the needs of the children they work with. I appreciate that the early years is often seen as a new profession, and that there are some who may question whether it is even seen as a profession at all due to its lack of a clear disciplinary core, but in my mind I picture a giant knowledges basket that every early years professional holds and can rummage through as they seek to meet the needs of the context. The knowledges basket is overflowing with multiple theoretical perspectives, including psychology, sociology, cultural theories, health, social policy, cultural studies and family studies, along with pedagogic knowledge that encompasses an appreciation of the different forms of play that exist, and workplace knowledge and (not forgetting) knowledge about forming relationships. However, the knowledges basket also contains knowledge of how to apply, combine and evaluate these knowledges, demonstrating that professionals are forever having to get a larger basket.

.... **CHAPTER SUMMARY**

- Early years in a theoretical hybrid, being a multi-disciplinary profession.
- The early years knowledge-base is more than just theory, encompassing pedagogic and everyday knowledge.
- Knowledge alone is not enough – professionals need to know how to combine knowledges to meet the needs of the context.
- There is no simple relationship between knowledge and skills.
- The application of knowledge is careful, skilful, complex work, combining knowledges to meet the needs of the context.

.... **FURTHER READING**

Campbell-Barr, V., Georgeson, J., Adams, H. and Short, E. (2018). *Child-Centredness in Practice: Report on Output 2*. Plymouth: Plymouth University. Available at: https://www.plymouth.ac.uk/uploads/production/document/path/11/11819/Report_02_Analysis_of_Observations_of_Child-Centred_Practice_in_European_Early_Childhood_Education_and_Care.pdf

This report is based upon observations of child-centred practice in six European countries. The report explores in detail what it means to be child-centred in practice, illustrating the ways in which knowledges come together to inform professional skills.

QAA (2014). *Subject Benchmark Statement: Early Childhood Studies*. Gloucester: The Quality Assurance Agency for Higher Education. Available at: www.qaa.ac.uk/docs/qaa/subject-benchmark-statements/sbs-early-childhood-studies-14.pdf?sfvrsn=fbe3f781_10

This document outlines what an Early Childhood Studies degree looks like in England. It might be that you want to find the equivalent document for your own context in order to analyse the knowledge and skills that are present within it.

5

CONCEPTS OF CHILDHOOD, FROM SELF TO SOCIETY

In earlier chapters I have explored that knowledge has different forms, structures and processes of legitimisation. Within these different kinds of knowledge are our own understandings of what childhood is. Our concepts of childhood will reflect not only individual experiences of childhood, but also observations of other childhoods that we encounter and broader social conceptions as to what childhood is (or should be). The individual and the social are not exclusive; in fact, they will be entwined in an intricate system of individual experiences and social norms. Therefore, in this chapter I want to consider what childhood is and how this is shaped by individual experiences of childhood and the society in which individuals live. I will also briefly consider the notion of a global childhood and the complexity of having common global constructions of childhood that are realised in both similar and different ways around the world.

What do You Think is Childhood?

The thing about childhood is that everyone has had one and this means that everyone 'knows' what childhood is, or at least what they have experienced childhood to be. Childhood experiences are an important part in framing personal understandings of what childhood is. Adults draw on their experiences to inform constructions of:

> ... where children 'should be' (at home/at school), what they 'should do', who they 'should be' with, whether they can decide about their lives for themselves, what is 'normal', that is, expected of them and so on. (Campbell-Barr and Bogatić, 2017: 1463)

Childhood experiences combine with social, historical, political and moral understandings of childhood to inform the ways in which professionals work with children and understandings of the role of early years services.

Every year when I work with students to reflect on their concepts of childhood I am struck by the similarities in their constructions of childhood. As Kehily (2010) writes, remembering childhood often calls to mind romantic adventures of play and fantasy and this is certainly evident amongst my students. Adults frequently recount romantic memories of childhood, fuelled by nostalgia (Willan, 2017), with an almost Famous Five feel to them. Whilst there are questions as to the accuracy of memories, what always interests me is how the romantic memories form as a basis on which early years professionals interpret their role and their understanding of early years services. For example, there seems to be a parallel between memories of outdoor play and a passion for providing outdoor learning experiences in the early years.

Whilst romantic memories are often at the core of influencing a professional's motivation to work in early years services, I am also all too aware that negative experiences in childhood may also inform professional practice. As such, professionals can want to protect children from the negative experiences that they encountered in childhood, striving to achieve a more romantic childhood for the children that they work with. Just as films and books can draw upon romantic imagery, they can also present counter-romantic images; the former seeks to provide a sense of comfort, whilst the latter challenges the audience and generates a sense of discomfort. The sense of comfort (or not) draws upon a commonality in constructions of childhood, which illustrates that the individual is deeply embedded in the social when considering concepts of childhood.

Experiences of childhood will be shaped by families, where an individual lives, the school attended, the media engaged with, etc. Childhood cannot be understood in isolation as it is embedded in class, gender, ethnicity and so on (Jenks, 2004). The combination of the individual and the social is not just in relation to the coming together of the private sphere of the family and the public world of media and education (for example), but also how the social influences constructions of childhood. Professionals need to consider what they understand childhood to be as it shapes them as a professional.

Understanding concepts of childhood is important for early years professionals as it shapes individual motivations for working with young children. Therefore, there is a need to engage with individual and social concepts of childhood to develop a deeper understanding of what informs and motivates professional early years practice. In many respects, concepts of childhood become a lens through which to view the knowledges and skills of early years professionalism.

QUESTION

What do you think constitutes a 'good' childhood? Analyse your ideas for evidence of where your own childhood has influenced your understanding.

World Views of Childhood

The experiential provides a commonsense meaning to childhood, drawn from experiences of being a child, having a child or other relationships with children (Jenks, 2004). Understandings of early years services come to be shaped by what we know, or at least assume to know, about children and childhood and what we, as adults, think children need. Knowledges of children and childhood will incorporate vertical discourse (with its varying structures) and horizontal discourse: the theoretical and the everyday (see Chapter 3). Our assumptions about children and what is a good childhood inform our world view, providing lenses with which to interpret the world. Our world view should not be confused with a universal view of childhood, rather our world view will be shaped by the meaning we have created for ourselves through our interactions with others (Jenks, 2004) as to what childhood is.

Whilst individual concepts of childhood are shaped by experiences, society also has a role in shaping what it is that we remember – the moments that are deemed noteworthy (Parker-Rees, 2015). For example, adults do not tend to recount childhood memories of getting dressed in the morning, but they may remember a special outfit worn at a party. The example reflects how it is the specialness of the party that makes the occasion noteworthy and that the everyday is often forgotten. The notion that we 'know' what childhood is, is grounded in a social, political, historical and even moral context (Jenks, 2004) that will inform what is deemed noteworthy. The specialness of a party holds resonance in a western construction of a relatively affluent childhood, but what of a child living in severe poverty or in a remote community in the rainforests of Brazil? Individual concepts of childhood are therefore distorted constructions of childhood, shaped by snapshots of experiences embedded in a particular context, as opposed to representing the actualities of childhood.

During professional training, theory and practice, as representations of knowledges and skills, will shape our world view on childhood, but our world views can also change with time. For example, the training undertaken to become an early years professional will introduce new knowledge that may influence a professional's world view. Di Santo et al. (2017) explored how post-secondary students in Canada come with particular beliefs about children, classroom practices and how to guide children's behaviour when entering pre-service early childhood education training. Training can either reaffirm or reject these beliefs, but time in practice will also alter individuals' behaviour and beliefs (see Chapter 7). The combination of theory and practice in early years training (see Chapter 2) represents how early years professional training provides options to develop one's world view of childhood.

People who work with children have strong views on childhood, but these are negotiated in relation to other views of childhood and other experiences of childhood. There are common constructions of childhood that reflect a collective understanding of childhood (a common world view), but we have to remember that these are adult views (Parker-Rees, 2015). There is an implied mirror between the adult and the child, whereby the child reflects what it is that the adult has constructed them to be. How adults construct a child and childhood is not the same as being a child (Uprichard, 2008). Adult concepts of childhood constitute a mix of different common constructs of childhood which reflect romantic, developmental and democratic perspectives that both contradict and complement each other in informing collective views of childhood – and early years professionals will negotiate their way between, around and within these different perspectives.

Romanticism

As discussed above, memories of childhood are often related to a romantic imagery, but romantic constructs of childhood are something of a perpetual myth, often not reflective of the time that gave rise to the construct. The romantic concept of childhood is attributed to Rousseau and his philosophy of the natural child (Gabriel, 2017). The romantic concept presents a view of the child as innocent, pure and natural, with a need for adult protection and guidance (Campbell-Barr, 2014). The natural child was a response to the severity of the industrial revolution and the predominant urban living. A desire to position children as distant from industrial and urban living gave rise to the natural image, whereby children were to be protected from the realities of the adult world. The long history of romanticism means that it is deeply ingrained in understandings of childhood and early years services (see Chapter 1).

Those who work with children are often motivated by a romantic concept of childhood, building on a view of children who need to be cared for and protected, offering them the freedom to explore and play (often within natural environments) in support of their natural development. However, there is a tension within romantic concepts of childhood between offering children freedom and a perceived need for protection, whereby an adult who provides a child too much freedom is one who neglects their role in protecting a child. For example, I have already raised the romantic image of outdoor play and providing children with the freedom to explore the natural environment, but there are limits to the freedom and the extent of explorations. An early years professional could not allow a child to walk to the woods on their own in most contexts as this would be seen as counter to their role to protect. Protection can therefore act as a limit to freedom, illustrating the contradictions present within adults' concepts of childhood and how professionals find themselves negotiating the different constructs (see Chapter 1).

Being and becoming

Romantic concepts of childhood have a strong association with the notion of allowing children to *be* children. The being child celebrates childhood as an important stage in its own right. The being child is often positioned in opposition to the becoming child, whereby the becoming child is an adult in the making (Uprichard, 2008). The becoming child reflects a construct of childhood as being a path to adulthood, informed by developmental perspectives of the immaturity of children. Developmental perspectives draw heavily on the biological differences between children and adults and imply a universality to the progression that all individuals will go through in life. Developmental psychology is predicated on children's naturalness, with a presumed linear progression (Jenks, 2004). Whilst developmentally and biologically there is a degree of certainty that all individuals will grow, the rate of growth and other physical changes do not occur at prescribed times, but at indicative times. The becoming child is therefore something of a myth as there is an implicit point at which an individual 'becomes' an adult, but it is this point that creates the mythical construction.

The mythical point at which an individual becomes an adult is well illustrated when looking at age signifiers. The becoming child imposes a temporality to childhood often indicated by signifiers of age whereby entry to adulthood is achieved on reaching a particular age that enables more 'adult' behaviours. For example, the age at which people can get married and legally have sex is a signifier of a distinction between childhood and adulthood. Prior to the given age, an individual child is considered too immature, but this immaturity changes after the given birthday. However, analysis of the age at which individuals can get married internationally illustrates the variable ways in which adults in different countries have constructed the distinction between adulthood and childhood. Further, there is no consensus on the age at which an individual enters adulthood when analysing legal requirements within a country. For example, in the UK, you can get married at 16, but you cannot drink alcohol at your wedding until you are 18. As Rosen (2007) explores, age is used politically within international laws but there are many factors that come into play in determining distinctions between childhood and adulthood.

Other signifiers are also incorporated into constructions of the becoming child. Language has been constructed as a symbol of knowing (Jenks, 2004). In particular, the ability to verbally articulate understanding is an important signifier, symbolised by the importance that adults place on a baby's first word. However, sociological perspectives of childhood have sought to highlight that it is not possible to distinguish when you become an adult. Not only does the becoming child impose a deficit view onto childhood and children, it also implies a day of enlightenment at which point an individual *becomes* an adult. However, given that adults can always learn from their experiences (see Chapter 7) then surely there is an element of which all individuals are in a continual process of becoming.

QUESTION

How would you define an adult? Have you become an adult?

There is a risk that children become rendered incompetent through the creation of artificial boundaries between childhood and adulthood. Uprichard (2008) proposes that if the temporality of childhood is rejected, children can be regarded as both being and becoming. The being child recognises childhood as an important stage in its own right, as opposed to solely a path to adulthood. The being child is grounded in democratic perspectives of childhood, whereby children are recognised as active social agents. Democratic perspectives of children's rights break the construction of an implied immaturity of children as unknowing. The democratic perspective also challenges a romantic protectionist construction that positions children as powerless and dependent. The recognition of children's agency acknowledges children's ability to act independently and to make free choices.

The democratic perspective of children with agency is compelling within the early years, reflected in the use of terms such as the 'competent child' or within the pedagogical knowledge of child-centred practice (see Chapter 4), whereby the centring of the child reflects democratic perspectives of children's rights. The United Nations Convention on the Rights of the Child (UNCRC) has undoubtedly been influential in raising the profile of children's rights and there are parallels between the rise of children's rights and the development of the sociology of childhood. The sociology of childhood sought to draw attention to both constructions of childhood and children's agency (Gabriel, 2017).

The democratic perspective is not solely about recognising children's social agency. In particular, the constructions within the UNCRC demonstrate that children's rights include three broad ideas of: the interests of the child, non-discrimination and respect for their views; or what is sometimes referred to as the three Ps: protection, provision and participation (Gabriel, 2017). The three Ps illustrate the potentially contradictory nature of the democratic perspective as there are questions as to whether a protectionist perspective can be combined with a participatory perspective. Whilst the protectionist perspective potentially limits children's autonomy, the participation perspective is potentially liberatory (Dillen, 2006). Again, the links to child-centred practice are evident within the parallels of child-centred being potentially liberatory, but within the confines of developmentalism (the becoming child). As outlined in Chapter 1, early years professionals find themselves negotiating between the different concepts of childhood and the potential tensions and contradictions that are present within the varying concepts.

Investment

The concept of investment draws upon the developmental perspective of the becoming child, but seeks to establish childhood as important through a notion of it being the foundation to children's lifelong learning. As outlined in Chapter 2, early years services have become synonymous with social investment strategies, whereby investment in early childhood is regarded as an investment in children's lifelong learning. The emphasis on quality and high returns as the basis for governments to invest in early years services shifts the developmental construct of the becoming child towards an economic construct, whereby the child is only valued on their reaching adulthood.

The normative construct of invest now (in young children and their education) and save later (as the child becomes a successful adult who requires minimal economic intervention from the state – see Chapter 2) places a monetary value onto childhood. Attempts to demonstrate the effectiveness of early years services have included economic value for money assessments. Research projects such as the Perry Preschool programme (also known as High Scope), the Abecedarian and the Chicago Child–Parent Centres are longitudinal studies that have assessed the economic returns of children attending early years services (Campbell-Barr, 2012). The economic returns consider both the advantages for the individual (higher earnings on entering adulthood) and for the state (a reduction in expenditure on welfare services). There are methodological questions about all of the studies, such as the sample sizes, how representative the samples are of all children, the influence of the projects taking place in American preschools and whether it is possible to economically assess *all* outcomes that early years services achieve (Penn, 2012b), but what is important to note is how universal the concept of investment has become (Campbell-Barr and Bogatić, 2017). However, here I am interested in what an economic assessment of early years services says about childhood.

The concept of investment creates childhood as an economic phase, where value can only really be achieved once adulthood is reached. Not only does the concept of investment devalue childhood (emphasising the becoming child), it also represents how adults are involved in a process of constructing what it is they *think* children need for the future. Investment is based upon a prediction of the future (Piper, 2008) – a best guess as to what knowledge, skills and other attributes children will need on their entering adulthood. As Heckman (2000) has raised, the guesswork is focused on academic performance and notions of school readiness, where socio-emotional domains become characterised as 'fluff'. Whilst school readiness is a much debated concept (Wickett, 2017), it indicates how childhood has become a series of preparations for the next stage. Early years is a preparation for primary school, primary school for secondary school, and so forth. Early years professionals thus become answerable to the next stage of childhood and the predictions of the future needs of children.

The concept of investment is often associated with the becoming child, whereby childhood is not only devalued based upon a view of children's perceived immaturity, but is also economically devalued. Economic constructs of childhood sit uneasily with romantic notions of childhood. The concept of investment is in tension with a more humanistic perspective of childhood and early years services that premise the social and emotional well-being of the child – where the 'being' emphasises the importance of the child in the here and now. Within the humanistic perspective there is a social, moral and ethical view of early years services that is far removed from the economics of investment (Campbell-Barr, 2014).

The concept of investment appears to be in opposition to romantic concepts of childhood. However, returning to the origins of the romantic concept of childhood, the desire to protect children from the industrialisation of urban areas included moves to prevent child labour. In the 19th century a succession of child labour laws – the Factory Acts – were passed to limit children's working hours. Children's position within society was shifted from one of being economic providers to being economically dependent. Additional laws, introduced around the same time, began the introduction of compulsory schooling (Hendrick, 1997). Thus, in a tale of twisted irony, it could be that the Romantic Movement gave rise to the concept of investment through the introduction of compulsory schooling.

Adult motivations in relation to children and childhood are often underpinned by a construction of the 'best interests of the child', such as work not being good, but education is. However, the question is which child's interests are all of these early years initiatives really for?

QUESTION

Return to you definition of a good childhood and consider where there are links to the concepts of romanticism, being and becoming and investment.

Global Childhood

Throughout the romantic, developmental (including economic) and democratic perspectives of childhood there is an implied universalism – a commonality to childhood. However, there are both challenges to the commonality and an appreciation for the ways in which the different perspectives are negotiated in different contexts. First, in considering the challenges to the presumed commonality of childhood is the challenge to the 'normal child' that forms the basis of developmental, and associated economic, perspectives. The normal child that shapes the rationale to invest in early years services is likely to be a western child (Tobin, 2005), with the adults' guesses as to what children will need for the future being bound by western perspectives. Childhood has become institutionalised based upon a presumed comprehensiveness and universality to what it is that adults determine children will need (Campbell-Barr and Bogatić, 2017). However, anyone who has ever travelled will tell you about the differences in how children live their lives. Even within a country such as the UK, there will be differences in the child-hood experiences of children living in London as opposed to those who live in the middle of Bodmin Moor in Cornwall. Not only will experiences vary, but so too will their needs. However, in recognising that childhood is anything but universal, I am also aware of the persuasiveness of developmentalism and the associated economic concept of childhood.

The criticisms of the economic concept of childhood risk being something of a west-ern privilege. I live in a country (Britain) where children are entitled to attend an early years setting from the age of three. I do not think that the provision of early years places is perfect, for example rates of funding could be improved and the pay, conditions and recognition for early years professionals could also be enhanced, but I can make chal-lenges to the system of funding early years provision as there is a system in place to be challenged. Not all countries have this.

Research from countries such as Bhutan (Pisani et al., 2017) and Jamaica (Kinkead-Clark, 2017) illustrates the different ways in which countries engage with the varying concepts of childhood as a result of the local context. For many countries (including Bhutan and Jamaica) there is an active engagement with, and promotion of, the concept of investment in a drive to increase investments in early years services. This does not mean that early years professionals are any less resistant to the concept of investment; as Kinkead-Clark (2017) explores in the Jamaican context, professionals are still nego-tiating different concepts of childhood and understandings of the role of early years services. However, within some countries there will be an active engagement with the concept of investment in an attempt to ensure access to early years services.

The United Nations' Sustainable Development Goals are a sharp reminder of the global differences in childhood. For example, within Goal 4 – *Ensure inclusive and equita-ble quality education and promote lifelong learning opportunities for all* – there are a number of targets and indicators, as shown in Table 5.1.

Table 5.1 Goal 4: Ensure inclusive and equitable quality education and promote lifelong learning opportunities for all

4.2	4.2.1
By 2030, ensure that all girls and boys have access to quality early childhood development, care and pre-primary education so that they are ready for primary education	Proportion of children under 5 years of age who are developmentally on track in health, learning and psychosocial well-being, by sex
	4.2.2
	Participation rate in organized learning (one year before the official primary entry age), by sex

Source: United Nations (2015)

The goal acts as a reminder that many children do not have access to early years (pre-primary) education and that often access to education is discriminated against on the grounds of gender. I do believe in the benefits of early years education, and I also believe that early years services offer far more benefits to children and families than will be captured by economic assessments; but what concerns me is how targets such as those stated in Goal 4 are realised in local contexts. The normative construct of early years services as a social investment strategy is evident within the Sustainable Development Goals, including reference to children being 'ready' for primary education. However, there is a question as to whether the 'readying' is merely a western concept of childhood, with a presumed normal child embedded in it, being imposed onto all contexts. As such, should early years services be universal in their structure, scope and aims or should there be real opportunities to develop more localised models?

The risk of a global convergence of ideas on early years services is well illustrated by the International Early Learning Study (IELS) (OECD, 2015a), dubbed the Baby PISA. The IELS will assess learning outcomes of children attending early years services in different countries in a similar way to the PISA studies (OECD, 2014). The parallels to the PISA studies have generated concern amongst those who believe that there should be more contextualised approaches to early years services (Moss et al., 2016). The PISA studies have illustrated how international comparisons of the educational performance of 15-year-old students in reading, mathematics and science can result in both positive and negative outcomes for education services at national levels. For countries such a Finland, who have performed well in the PISA tests, there has been the generation of PISA tourism and an international reputation for their educational model (Marshall, 2014). However, for countries that perform less well there can be dramatic changes to their education systems, which whilst potentially generating greater investment, also illustrate how educational models can be adapted as a result of a decontextualised test (McNess et al., 2015). A further risk is present whereby those countries who do not perform well seek to uncritically adopt or mimic the educational models of those who have performed well, developing decontextualised approaches to education.

The potential convergence of ideas on what childhood should look like is not just in relation to educational services. Rosen (2007) explores the emotive issue of child soldiers and efforts by humanitarian organisations to end the use of child combatants. The calls to end child soldiers are grounded in democratic perspectives of children's rights and what Rosen (2007) refers to as the 'Straight 18' position, whereby a single international standard of childhood is established, potentially at the expense of competing (local) definitions. The humanitarian arguments within the Straight 18 campaign clash with any local perspectives on the involvement of children in war. Potentially, the humanitarian interpretation of children's rights positions children as dependent and powerless, denying any choice to engage in combat or that combat actually proffers active participation in society. Rosen (2007) draws on anthropological perspectives to illustrate how the lived experiences of children who participate in war can be one of empowerment. The debates on child soldiers echo those within the Sustainable Development Goals, whereby there are questions as to whether humanitarian efforts impose particular constructs of childhood onto all contexts.

━━━━━━━━ QUESTION ━━━━━━━━

Do you think that humanitarian perspectives impose a western construct of childhood onto all contexts?

Multiplicities of Childhood

The risk with concepts of childhood is that they become a series of binaries: being or becoming, protection or participation, investment or humanism. However, rather than a series of binaries, structured as being in opposition and competition with each other, Gabriel (2017) explores the idea of multiplicities. Multiplicities allow for a range of events and processes that cross disciplinary boundaries in forming concepts of childhood. Thus, rather than developmental perspectives being based on either biology, psychology or (even) sociology, there is a multi-disciplinarity that draws together the different approaches to understanding childhood.

Multiplicities of childhood fit well with the multiple theoretical perspectives that shape and inform the work of early years professionals. As already outlined in Chapter 4, early years is a profession that draws upon a range of theoretical perspectives, along with varying forms of knowledge (from the theoretical to the everyday) to inform the early years professional knowledge-base. Understanding childhood as multiplicities thus continues the recognition that the early years is a rich profession that draws upon multiple perspectives.

An appreciation for the multiplicities perspective does create a potential challenge for early years professionals, because (as discussed in Chapter 1) early years professionals become the meeting point for different perspectives on childhood. Whilst I have discussed the idea of early years professionals having to negotiate between the different perspectives, the notion of multiplicities provides a richness of ideas with which to inform professional practice. Therefore, rather than concepts of childhood being something that early years professionals have to juggle, they become something to add to the richness of the early years professional knowledge-base, offering endless opportunities to develop the ways in which professionals work with children.

Conclusion

I appreciate that the notion of multiplicities of childhood might be potentially overwhelming, contradictory and even (overly) optimistic. The world view of any early years professional on childhood will be located within particular contexts, where there can be pressures to secure funding for early years services or pressures to ensure children are school ready, and where the definition of readiness is confined to academic ability.

However, I think that it is important to appreciate what one's world view is, where it has come from and how it relates to other broader concepts of childhood, as this will enhance professional understanding as to why it is that some issues surrounding childhood make us feel comfortable, whilst others generate a sense of discomfort.

Multiplicities of childhood enable an appreciation that there is no universal childhood – a singular way to experience childhood, nor a singular way with which to work with children. In many respects, multiplicities emphasise the role of early years professionals in responding to the world views of policy makers, parents and even the children they work with. However, it is important to remember that these are adult world views, so maybe now is the time to consider children's concepts of childhood.

CHAPTER SUMMARY

- There are common concepts of childhood that shape the ways in which adults think childhood 'should' be and what children 'should' be doing.
- Concepts of childhood have evolved over time, but the emergence of new ideas does not mean that the old ones go away.
- Concepts of childhood can be internally conflicted, whereby a concept such as romanticism offers the conflicting opportunities of childhood liberation and childhood protection.
- Concepts of childhood often conflict with each other, creating a scenario whereby early years professionals have to mediate between the different concepts of childhood.
- There is a risk that the global interest in early years services is resulting in a convergence of ideas about how early years services should be provided and what their role is, potentially decontextualising the role of the early years professional.
- Early years professionals need to consider their world view of childhood and analyse how it shapes their work with young children.

FURTHER READING

The NSPCC – Legal definition of child rights: https://www.nspcc.org.uk/preventing-abuse/child-protection-system/legal-definition-child-rights-law/legal-definitions/

The NSPCC (National Society for the Prevention of Cruelty to Children) is a UK organisation that believes every childhood is worth fighting for. This web page provides an overview of different legal ages that distinguish between childhood and adulthood in the UK and internationally. Consider the different ages and their implications for when (or if) childhood ends.

Uprichard, E. (2008). 'Children as "being and becomings": children, childhood and temporality', *Children and Society*, 22(4), 303–13.

This is a well-written article exploring the contradictions between the concept of children as being and/or becoming, proposing that children can be seen as both, thus offering an example of bringing together different concepts of childhood.

6

EMOTIONAL
KNOWLEDGE

In this chapter I want to consider the knowledges that are beyond that which is considered theoretical knowledge or vertical discourse with its varying structures (see Chapter 3). I want to consider knowledges that sit outside of that which is traditionally described as knowledge. There is a variable language with which to describe this knowledge, whereby it is referred to interchangeably as attitudes, beliefs, dispositions and an ethic of care. The variable language creates a challenge as to how best to refer to this knowledge and how to explore what it constitutes. I therefore use 'emotionology' as a shorthand to explore the terms attitudes, beliefs, dispositions and an ethic of care and what lies within them. I consider what constitutes emotionology, focusing particularly on love and its place within early years professionalism (and that of teaching), but as I go through the chapter it will be evident that emotionology is about more than just love.

The Origins of the Profession

For all the discussion of technocratic models of professionalism (see Chapter 2) and the tying of professionalism to a knowledge-base, there is much to suggest that the origins of the profession are more philosophically (and romantically) orientated. As discussed in Chapter 3, Durkheim was a sociologist who identified the origins of the profession as being shaped by a spiritual, moral and ethical framework. Specifically, professionalism had its origins in religion, with the first professions of priesthood, medicine and law requiring that the technical activities of the professions were shaped by a socially expected morality (Grace, 2014). A professional was to have specialised knowledge within the moral framework of a pursuit for the common good. However, the Enlightenment, as a philosophical and cultural movement, emphasised individualism and reason, giving rise to more technocratic models of professionalism.

The moral basis to professionalism is evident within the early years. The work of Pestalozzi, Montessori and Froebel emphasised love as the foundation to supporting a child's learning. As Aslanian (2015) explores, Pestalozzi regarded love as the foundation to a child's moral, intellectual and spiritual development, whilst Froebel emphasised love and care in supporting children's unfolding nature. Montessori also explored how love was more than just caresses and affection, as professionals are to feel a child's spirituality. Whilst all three theorists seemed to draw upon a maternalistic construction of love, there is some evidence to suggest that this is not necessarily female; instead the maternal is symbolic of the relationship that is to be formed between the professional and the child (Aslanian, 2015). However, the three theorists each signify the origins of the profession as being more spiritual than technocratic.

Whilst the origins of the profession might be grounded in a construction of love, there is a complex tangle of socio-historic practices within the early years (see Chapter 1) that have seen shifting constructions of the place of love. The loving ideal of early years professionalism has clear associations with the Romantic Movement (see Chapters 1 and 5). However, whilst the Romantic Movement was (in part) a resistance to modernism and the Enlightenment, modernist perspectives favoured rationality and reason over the irrationality of emotions. Western modernist constructions of knowledge tend to be narrowly focused on knowledge and skills, whereby epistemological hierarchies privilege knowledge with a hierarchical structure (see Chapter 3). Instrumental rationality has been at the expense of morality in the development of techniques that guide professionals (Dahlberg and Moss, 2005). Consequently, emotions remain something that are recognised as being at the core of people, but are largely regarded as 'out there' rather than central to the profession.

Often emotions are marginalised through both a favouring of hierarchical knowledge and the creating of a series of binaries where one item is favoured over the other, such as male over female, rational over irrational, public over private, reason over emotion (Andrew, 2015). As I have already outlined in Chapters 1 and 5, such binary approaches have largely been rejected through recognition of a more intricate relationship between the items, but, for a time, there was a lasting legacy that resulted in emotions being marginalised from constructions of professionalism.

Sociological approaches illustrate that enactments of emotions are not internal reactions, nor 'out there', but patterns of action that are developed through social experiences (Andrew, 2015). Often emotions are regarded as individual, but they are a product of social interaction (Johnson, 2000). Emotive reactions illustrate the interaction with the other. The other can be a person or an object, but there is a shared, social interaction, whereby we understand emotions in relation to others (Maier-Höfer, 2015). For example, there are expected reactions that have been socially constructed, such as the ways in which one responds to a child who is crying. The patterns of action are what enable individuals to know whether a person is upset, scared, happy, etc.

The concepts of emotional labour and emotional capital illustrate both how emotions can be learnt and how it is possible to learn to use emotions within professional contexts. Emotional labour is attributed to the work of Hochschild (2003) and outlines how individuals regulate their emotions, expressing them in particular ways, in order to meet the requirements of the workplace. Within emotional labour, the emotions of individuals can be exchanged within the marketplace – they become a commodity to be bought and sold. However, there is an underlying exploitative aspect to emotional labour whereby employers use the emotions of employees in order to sell a service of some kind. For example, a waitress might not feel happy, but they will convey the emotion of happiness in order to make the experience of being in a restaurant more enjoyable for the customer and to fulfil the expectations of their employer.

Conversely, emotional capital, which stems from the work of Bourdieu (2008), explores how rather than emotions being exploited within the labour market, positioning them as a form of capital provides the opportunity for an individual to create profit from them. As capital, emotions are identified as having a value (Andrew, 2015) rather than marginalised. For both emotional labour and emotional capital, individuals need to be aware of their emotions and to actively use these in order for them to form part of a commodified transaction. However, within emotional capital, emotions and emotion work become visible both economically and culturally, recognised as a part of the knowledges needed by early years professionals in dealing with the complexities of working with young children (Andrew, 2015).

For early years professionals, it is evident that the origins of the profession as grounded in emotions are still pertinent, illustrated in the centrality of the interaction with the other – the early years professional with the child. The resistance to technocratic models of professionalism illustrates a dissatisfaction with the notion of professionalism being based upon a series of identifiable, observable items (see Chapter 2). The focus on that which can be identified and observed within professionalism has resulted in a loss and devaluing of that which is assumed to be too hard to identify and observe (Held, 2002). Emotions, grounded in a more moral and philosophical framework of professionalism, have become marginalised, resulting in the challenges of how best to describe this 'out there' knowledge. Within the literature there is evidence of the use of attitudes, beliefs, dispositions and an ethic of care all being used to help illustrate the knowledge of emotions.

Attitudes are often associated with beliefs, whereby individuals have particular beliefs about ideas, things and people. Attitudes represent a particular way of thinking about things, an enduring belief that can offer an evaluative function (Georgeson and Campbell-Barr, 2015). The embedded beliefs become a set of personal, complex and self-fulfilling ideas that provide a lens through which professionals view their role (Hedges and Cullen, 2005). Beliefs represent the implicit theories that professionals hold, drawn from their academic knowledge and personal experiences. Beliefs are personal, self-fulfilling and frequently inconsistent (Brock, 2013), but nonetheless are an important influence on how professionals understand their role and how they undertake it. Attitudes (and their embedded beliefs) therefore act as a pre-disposition. A disposition represents a tendency to behave in a particular way, a pattern of behaviour and a habit of mind that is intentional. However, attitudes as a pre-disposition imply that there is no action.

The ethic of care can be regarded as a return to the origins of the profession due to its underlying moral focus. The morality is more than following universal ethical codes with predefined rights and wrongs (Dahlberg and Moss, 2005). It should not be confused with a saintly-type image of an early years professional who knows all the rights and wrongs. The focus on an ethic of care is about recognising the moral responsibility for the other.

An ethic of care derives from feminist work around caring, emphasising the ethical responsibility that is embedded within caring, whereby one puts the other before oneself and there is an engrossment in the other (Noddings, 2012). The focus on an ethic of care is also a challenge to modernity and the privileging of scientific rationality over other knowledges and the underlying implied pursuit of uniformity of thought and practice.

> Scientific knowledge and instrumental rationality gain prominence at the expense of other types of knowledge and rationality, their hegemony expressed in the singular terms of 'reason' and 'knowledge' and the strangeness to the ear of the plural 'reasons' and 'knowledges'.
> (Dahlberg and Moss, 2005: 55)

An ethic of care is relational and inter-subjective, again emphasising the social nature of the profession. The social inter-subjectivity of emotions emphasises that there is a focus on the other, but as illustrated earlier, the other is not necessarily the child. There is, therefore, a question as to who or what emotions are being directed towards. Much of the literature implies that the other is the child, emphasising the emotional relationship between the early years professional and the child, but it is also important to emphasise that the other can be the profession. As such, one may speak of a love of the job for example, expressing emotion towards the professional role as much as the interactions that take place within it. Therefore, as I explore the possible array of emotions that may inform professionalism in the early years, it is important to consider who or what they are being directed towards.

Emotionology

Emotionology: the attitudes or standards that a society, or definable group within a society, maintains toward basic emotions and their appropriate expression; ways that institutions reflect and encourage these attitudes in human conduct, e.g., courtship practices as expressing the valuation of affect in marriage, or personal workshops as reflecting the valuation of anger in job relationships. (Stearns and Stearns, 1985: 813)

The term emotionology is a useful shorthand for referring to the knowledges that I am discussing. The quote above is important in raising two points. The first is that often emotions are associated with romantic relationships, and as will be seen, discussions of love within professional contexts such as the early years have been hampered by a confusion in the use of the word love. The association between love and marriage has created a misplaced concern that love implies a sexualised relationship, tapping into moral panics around paedophilia (Loreman, 2011; Page, 2018). Whilst I will go on to explore love in more detail later, here it is important to stress that emotionology is in no way sexualised when used in the context of early years professionalism.

The second point to raise is that the quote refers to 'anger in job relationships' and whilst I hope early years professionals do not feel anger in their roles, it is worth noting that often emotionology within early years professionalism focuses on what might be referred to as positive emotions. Whilst Goldstein (1998) has raised that enactments of emotions are more than just smiles and hugs, there is an underlying assumption that the early years professional will be happy and smiling in their work. However, it is important to recognise the challenges of working in the early years, and at times not all emotions will be positive. Working with young children can involve coping with sick, wee, hitting, biting, tantrums, etc., which can understandably invoke negative emotions as much as laughing, playing, cuddling and seeing children develop can invoke positive emotions. Therefore, whilst much of the discussion is focused on positive emotions, I appreciate that there may be days when the emotionology is not fully positive.

Emotions are important to early years professionals (Van Laere et al., 2012), but the detail as to which emotions and what they look like is limited (Elfer, 2015). For example, Brodin et al. (2015), in research with those working with young children, found that professionals in Austria and Sweden (and to a lesser extent Bulgaria) thought that their attitude was important for the quality of services, but there is little discussion as to what is meant by 'attitude'. In Italy, a caring attitude has been identified as important by those undertaking their professional training (Balduzzi, 2011), but again there is a lack of exploration as to what is meant by the term caring.

In work undertaken with colleagues in Hungary and Italy, I was involved in a research project exploring interpretations of the term 'attitude' by tutors and students on early years degrees (Campbell-Barr, 2017b; Campbell-Barr et al., 2015). In the research we identified an array of items that tutors and students used to describe appropriate attitudes for working with young children. We did not look at the frequency of the words, but instead grouped them into four areas of Emotional Competence, Political Competence, Pedagogic Competence and Professional Competence. The focus on competence was not about creating a list of identifiable attitudes, nor an Anglo-American interpretation of competence as 'good enough' (see Chapter 2), but an attempt to open up a discussion of what is understood by attitudes within the context of early years professionalism.

Political competence reflected a need for professionals to be aware of the policy context, particularly in England where there had been a period of sustained policy intervention and change at the time of the research (see Chapter 1). Pedagogic competence related to the creation of the pedagogic environment, with an emphasis on a child-centred philosophy (see Chapter 4), whilst professional competence related to teamwork, reflective practice and a commitment to continued professional development. The political, pedagogic and professional competences therefore illustrate how the object of emotions can be variable from policy to the environment to a focus on the profession itself. However, it was within emotional competence that we found the largest range of terms: patience, enthusiasm, compassion, affection, love, caring, emotional connection with the child and personal disposition to want to work with children. Within emotional competence, the object of focus was the child and expressions of appropriate (and anticipated) emotional responses towards children.

In another piece of research, I analysed European literature for further evidence of the 'attitudes' needed to work with young children (see Figure 6.1). The terms, for me, reflect the importance of emotionology within early years professionalism. The terms are not necessarily universal, as the earlier research had already illustrated to me how those training to work with young children will variably identify with the terms depending on the cultural context that they are in (Campbell-Barr, 2017b; Campbell-Barr et al., 2015). Early years professionals will variably align themselves to the different terms in response to cultural expectations as to how professionals should 'be' and what is deemed the appropriate vocabulary with which to describe that 'being'. The terms are therefore not mutually exclusive, but interrelated, and what one professional, in one particular cultural context, might describe as 'love', another may say is being 'emotionally open'.

Social understandings of children and early years professionalism are a powerful force in shaping the knowledges for working with young children. The vocabulary to describe emotions might vary within different cultural contexts, but so too will the enactments of those emotions. In a survey with early years professionals working in New Zealand, Dalli (2008) found that respect for children, being fair and developing trust were identified as underpinning pedagogic approaches. Included in the analysis are details as to what this might look like in practice, such as getting down to the child's level, using

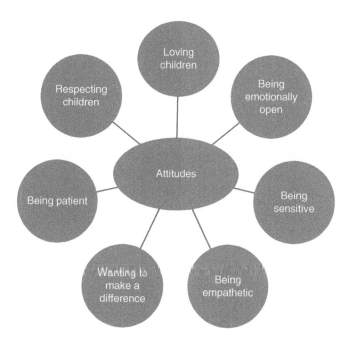

Figure 6.1 Attitudes for working with children

open ended questions, providing greetings and farewells and having responsive interactions. There is a risk that the identification of attitudes and associated understandings of what they might look like in practice results in creating a checklist as to whether an early years professional encompasses (and embodies) all of these behaviours. Any attempt at a checklist would therefore undermine an appreciation of the complexity of how professionals come to know appropriate emotional responses. Whilst there are anticipated social understandings of emotional responses in given situations, the exactness of the response is not prescribed, because there will be a range of knowledges being combined to shape the emotional response.

═══════════ **QUESTION** ═══════════

Consider the terms in Figure 6.1. What would you add to or take away from them to describe the attitudes needed to be an early years professional?

As discussed in Chapter 3, professionals will select and apply knowledges to varying extents to meet the needs of the context. For example, even the age of the child and the perception of their needs will mould the ways in which a professional selects the various knowledges (including emotional ones) to inform their professional practice. Instead, the terms identified with the discussion of emotionology are designed to open up an examination as to what emotionology might look like within early years professionalism. As 'attitudes', the terms symbolise the lenses through which professionals understand their professional role, whilst providing an evaluative function for how they enact it.

The Learning of Emotions

The variable terminology used to describe emotionology, along with the various emotions that are described within it, may be the result of the different theoretical perspectives that have been adopted to explore emotions. Loreman (2011), in exploring the notion of *Love as Pedagogy* within educational contexts, identifies how love has been explored from biological, neurological, spiritual, religious and philosophical perspectives. Whilst some of the perspectives seek to offer a scientification of love, others can be regarded as more fluid and open in their approach. However, the underlying rationale is that love (and other emotions) forms an important basis with which to support children's development (Loreman, 2011).

Western perspectives on the emotional responses of adults to children have been dominated by attachment theory. Whilst attachment theory might be criticised for the presumed normality of child development embedded within it and for prescribing what a 'good' attachment looks like, there are aspects of the theory that reflect the ethic of care. Attachment requires a person who is responsive to the child and allows the child to feel secure (Bowlby, 1958; Bowlby et al., 1956), but there are different layers to attachment. Therefore, whilst attachments between early years professionals and the children they work with have been established as being important, less is known about what the attachment might look like (Page, 2018).

The Key Person Approach in England represents one model that signifies an emotional relationship between a child and a professional. Within this approach children are allocated a professional who is intended to be their primary 'go to' person. However, my own experience of sending my son to nursery was that the person who was allocated as his Key Person was not the same professional as the one he had the strongest emotional relationship with. Thus the paper exercise of allocating Key People may not be the same as the relationships that form within the early years environment. As discussed in Chapter 4, knowing about the importance of attachment is not enough to enable an individual to form attachments – the knowledge alone will not meet the needs of the context and ensure professional practice. Thus the theoretical analysis of attachments and emotions more generally has sought to establish their importance, but done little to explore the complexities of forming emotional relationships within professional contexts.

In feminist work exploring the emotional connection between adults and the children they are working with, there is recognition that the use of a term such as love is illustrative of a commitment, alongside an implied intimacy and loyalty. Noddings has explored how the caring relationship is about putting the other before oneself and engrossing in the other (Noddings, 2010, 2012). Caring brings the other forth, whilst teaching implies a distancing.

Goldstein (1998) has undertaken research to help illustrate the intricacies of the emotional relationships that professionals form with the children they work with. Goldstein emphasises the ethical, philosophical and experiential roots of caring, arguing that they are more than mere personality traits. Drawing on participant observations undertaken with a primary grade teacher in America, Goldstein details the careful ways in which the teacher mediates the expectations of her as a professional and the needs of the children in her class. Consideration of the needs of the children in the class highlights how professionals are required to make decisions about those needs (such as the notion of in the best interests of the child discussed in the previous chapter). The needs of the children are balanced against the needs of the professional, the curriculum, the policy context, etc., demonstrating how the early years professional draws on their knowledges to do so (although I recognise this is my interpretation). Whilst the emphasis is placed on the other (the one being cared for), Noddings refers to the reciprocity in the relationship, whereby it is recognised that both the one cared for and the one caring have needs which are to be met.

Andrew (2015) also acknowledges the role of the social in shaping appropriate enactments of emotions when working with young children. Emotional enactments will be developed and refined through the interaction with the other and wider social experiences. Andrew offers the example of learning to be empathetic, whereby a professional is learning an appropriate response to a child's circumstances. Empathy requires that an individual can reconstruct another individual's experience. Empathy is not just the response, but also how the social and the individual combine to shape that response (Andrew, 2015). The focus on empathy illustrates my emphasis on knowledges, whereby the professional requires knowledge of the child's circumstances, knowledge of how those circumstances relate to other children (such as being better or worse off) and knowledge of how to act and respond appropriately to the child. The knowledge combinations also illustrate the coming together of individual and world views of what childhood is or at least should be. The application of the knowledges will involve a process of trial and error, whereby professionals will adapt their responses daily in pursuit of refined professional practice.

The cultural variations in the terms used to describe emotional responses are evident when contrasting Andrew's Australian study with work undertaken by Rajala and Lipponen (2018) in Finland. In the Finnish context, Rajala and Lipponen (2018) advocate a focus on compassion, whereby compassion is also identified as a social response based upon the feelings of another. Compassion represents a moral response to the suffering of another and their experiences, prompting an empathetic concern (Lipponen et al., 2018). The empathetic concern illustrates the related nature of the terms used within the emotionology alongside the cultural variances in how to describe the emotional aspects of working with young children.

As discussed, emotions are understood within social contexts, developed through experiences with others and representative of dominant ideals. Research conducted with those studying at below degree level to work with young children has suggested that those working with children often identify their work as requiring innate characteristics (Skeggs, 1997; Vincent and Braun, 2011). Caring for the other is often constructed as a natural ability and aligned with femininity, whereby women are positioned as natural carers due to their biological ability to have children. Not only does the innate construct of caring build on arbitrary binaries that potentially exclude men from caring (see Chapter 1), it also hides the complexities of learning to care and the intricacies of emotional responses. To say that emotionology is tacit and embodied de-intellectualises the challenges of learning appropriate emotional responses. The recognition of the social context illustrates how individuals are given constant messages about right and wrong behaviours and right and wrong emotional interactions in forming the professional self.

Research undertaken by Colley (2006) illustrates how there is a constructed ideal of someone who works with young children. Again looking at those studying below degree level, Colley identifies something of a hidden curriculum whereby individuals are expected to align themselves to the ideal. Appropriate (and expected) behaviours are developed through participation on a training course, whereby both tutors and other students, alongside time in practice, form part of the process of providing messages about right and wrong behaviours.

Rekalidou and Panitsides (2015) undertook a survey with 150 university students in Greece to consider the knowledge, skills and attitudes they hoped to develop from participating in their degrees. The findings illustrated that the students placed a premium on personality traits. However, the study also acknowledged that all training was involved in a process of seeking to mould the beliefs of the students participating on it. It is to be expected that studying and training will involve a process whereby one learns to align oneself to the expected professional ideals. However, I do think that there is a need to be more open and explicit (perhaps even honest) in acknowledging the construction of the ideals. As I explored in Chapter 4, students might know what the ideal is, such as in the example of being a loving pedagogue in Hungary, but knowing how to meet that ideal is less than certain.

Participation in training as being sufficient for the acquisition of the required emotionology implies a hidden curriculum, whereby norms, values and expected behaviours are transmitted via the social environment of the training provision, but not openly acknowledged (and potentially not intended). I therefore think that tutors also need to acknowledge their place in the construction of the ideal early years professional, as do early years professionals themselves, in order to understand the implied emotionology that is present.

══════════ **QUESTION** ══════════

How would you describe the 'ideal' early years professional? What hidden emotionology is present within it?

Conclusion

There is still more work to be done on understanding the early years professional emotionology in order to fully understand what it is and how it is acquired. In considering what knowledge is (see Chapter 3), the distributing and testing of knowledge is key to supporting a process of scrutiny. True professionalism depends on a continued commitment to hold knowledge up to scrutiny, wherever it comes from and whatever its form (Furlong, 2000). Articulating an early years professional emotionology is therefore a first step in recognising the emotional knowledges of early years professionals. Some of the articulation has begun, but further work to cross-analyse the use of terms and what they mean is needed.

I would include within the identification of an early years professional emotionology, as a part of the early years knowledge-base, recognition of how professionals have to learn the knowledge and apply it. It is evident that working with young children requires more than just modernist, technocratic constructions of knowledge and skills. Emotionology brings together beliefs, attitudes, dispositions and an ethic of care, whereby beliefs represent the ideas an individual holds that form a particular way of thinking about things – their attitude and pre-disposition – that are then actioned through a pattern of mind that is intentional, representing the dispositional. However, the focus on an ethic of care represents how within emotionology, the dispositional is about behaviours towards another. The inter-subjective nature of an ethic of care emphasises the social nature of early years professionalism, both in relation to how there is a focus on the other (the child) and that there are learnt social expectations as to how the interaction with the other should be enacted.

I think it is important to emphasise the learnt aspect of emotionology in order to value emotions. The value is not in an economic sense of emotions as a commodity to be bought and sold, but in regard to valuing both the rich and varied ways that early years professionals know how to work with children and the complexities and intricacies of acquiring the knowledges for early years professionalism.

CHAPTER SUMMARY

- The origins of the profession are in a socially expected morality.
- Emotional responses are learnt through interactions with others and being a part of the cultural context, alongside participation in training.
- Emotions are inter-subjective, whereby there is a focus on the other. The other is typically a child within early years professionalism, but can also be the profession or something else.
- Emotionology represents the variable ways in which the emotional aspects of working with children are described, such as beliefs, attitudes, dispositions and an ethic of care.
- Within the early years professional emotionology there is a diverse vocabulary for describing the emotions required for working with young children, with terms being variably interpreted and utilised depending on the cultural context.

FURTHER READING

Andrew, Y. (2015). 'What we feel and what we do: emotional capital in early childhood work', *Early Years*, 35(4), 351–65.

This paper is particularly good at exploring the distinction between knowledge, skills and attitudes through drawing on the philopsophical terms of episteme, techne and phronesis. The paper also draws attention to the learning of attitudes/phronesis.

Campbell-Barr, V. (2018). *Cross Cultural Research in the Training of Early Childhood Educators*. Available at: http://methods.sagepub.com/video/cross-cultural-research-in-the-training-of-early-childhood-educators

In this short video I reflect on my experiences of undertaking research into the Hungarian cultural idea of a 'child loving adult'. Whilst I talk about some of the methodological challenges, I also explore the importance of considering the meanings of the terms that we use. Therefore, if you use terms such as 'love' to describe your professional role, what do you mean by them and what does this look like in practice?

7

LEARNING IN PRACTICE

In this chapter I want to focus on the interplay between knowledge and experience, particularly the place of experience in generating knowledges. In considering the place of experience, I turn to reflective practice as a way in which to both articulate practice and support the process of coming to know from experience. As such, I consider the notion of everyday knowledge (see Chapter 3) and how it is that experiential knowledge becomes an important part of the early years knowledge-base.

Knowledge and Experience

In Chapter 2, I outlined how most early years initial training courses combine practical training with that of taught sessions. The general acceptance of combining theory and practice in initial training reflects that there is a need for both in becoming an early years professional. The use of 'theory' and 'practice' as two separate terms obscures the relationship between the two rather than clarifying what the balance between them might look like (Young and Muller, 2014). Theory risks being positioned as too abstract and too distant from the professional to have any real meaning, whilst the lived experience of practice supports it in feeling more real and meaningful (see Chapter 2). However, despite the immediacy of experience, it is important that theory and practice are not seen as separate, but deeply entwined (see Chapter 3).

The relationship between theory and practice is, to an extent, circular, whereby professionalism is the applying of knowledge to meet the needs of the context (i.e. practice), but the application of knowledge within the context could give rise to new knowledge (i.e. theory). Whilst practice could generate new theory, experiential knowledges will have different structures to those of established theory (see Chapter 3). Pure knowledge (theory) develops conceptually and applied knowledge (practice) develops contextually. Further, the processes for distributing and validating the different knowledges will also contribute to the varying structures. However, it is not just the context of the early years that generates applied, practical knowledge as there are different layers to experiential knowledge.

Most people will have an empirical theory of how the world is based on observations and experiences (Winch, 2004). As outlined in Chapter 5, individuals possess a world view through which they interpret their early years professionalism, with this view being obtained through experiences and observations made in life both prior to and during professional practice. For example, Johnson (2000) outlines how individuals have a lot of knowledge just from being a part of a culture, such as having knowledge of words, the culturally appropriate ways in which to use those words and the social and cultural rules of when to use words and in what procedure. As such, if you ask an individual to tell you a story there is an anticipated structure to that story. Therefore, the experiences and observations that shape a professional's world view are not restricted to the specifics of an early years knowledge-base, instead being much broader in the generating of knowledges.

An early years professional's empirical theory of the world will be based upon different layers of observations and experiences. Some of the theory will not be specific to the early years, such as what is childhood, as everyone will have a view on what childhood is based on their experiences and observations. However, the example of considering what childhood is illustrates how being an early years professional provides an additional layer to the interpretation of childhood that will have been refined through the experiences of working directly with children and the observations made whilst doing so. There is therefore the general layer of observations and experiences that anyone can have, with the additional layer gained through being a part of the early years community.

Recognising the general layer and its distinction from that of being a part of the early years community helps to develop an understanding of how an individual manages the experience of their first day in an early years setting. For example, I can remember walking into a day nursery for the first day of a placement and the manager had been called away to deal with an incident at another nursery. With no one to guide me on what to do, I went to sit with the children on the carpet area and began to play with the Stickle Bricks that a girl had out in front of her. My general layer of knowledge guided me in going to sit and play, potentially generated through my own experiences of being in nursery, but over time, my participation within the early years community helped me to refine my early years empirical theory through my observations and experiences of being within the day nursery.

Socio-cultural theories are attributed to the work of Vygotsky and broadly recognise learning as being embedded in social events and interactions with others, objects and the environment. It is not my intention to go into depth about socio-cultural theories within the confines of this chapter, but to instead draw attention to how human development is embedded in the social, cultural and historical context (for further reading see Veraksa and Sheridan, 2018). For example, the analogy of knowing how to tell a story discussed earlier reflects how being a part of a community and interacting with others supports the use of language in appropriate ways. In a similar way, my participation in the nursery supported a process of learning appropriate ways to interact with the children.

The notion of learning through interacting with others is not uncommon within the early years as it is a recognised, important part of children's development. However, learning as a social process is also true of professional development. Lave and Wenger (1991) have extended socio-cultural theories to consider how learning is a process of participation through the concept of a community of practice. A community of practice recognises learning as a social process, whereby individuals are shaped by (and shape) the communities they are in. Members of the community build up a shared body of knowledge that can inform practice. The knowledge is not about technocratic approaches to practice (see Chapter 2), but a more philosophical sharing of ideas on how to approach practice. Newcomers are inducted into practice at the peripheries of the community and, over time, through participation in the community (or a process of legitimate peripheral participation) they move towards full participation (and mastery) (Payler and Locke, 2013). The participants are both changed by and change the practice.

Participation in practice does not solely support a tacit spreading of knowledge, whereby simply participating in practice will somehow guarantee the acquisition of the required knowledges. Instead, the participation is about an active process of 'doing'. Dewey was an American educational reformer who was concerned with interactions and social transactions and identified experience as central to the learning process. Dewey identified experience as the transaction of living organisms, whereby the 'doing' within the context provided learning opportunities (Biesta, 2014). For example, individuals learn about the consequences of their actions through the 'doing' of the action. In Chapter 6, I discussed how an attitude is a pre-disposition. A pre-disposition could also be regarded as a hypothesis as it is only after action that it can be regarded as knowledge. The action stops knowledge from being 'out there', disembodied from the knower or an object waiting to be discovered, and becomes contextual.

Empirical theory generated through observations and experiences of working within the early years is an important part of the early years professional knowledge-base. Within early years professionalism the experiences are both those that come from participating in the early years community and those gained through active participation (the doing of practice) in that community. However, there is a need to be cautious in relying too much on experiences, for a number of reasons. Firstly, if an early years professional were to only rely on their empirical theory generated through early years practice, the underlying assumption is that they would be at their most knowledgeable on the day that they retired. Any implied positive correlation between time and knowing masks the ebbs and flows of professional knowledge and that an individual sense of knowing can be high one day and low the next.

Secondly, relying too much on experiential knowledge could risk knowledge stagnating. Relying solely on experiential knowledge implies that all the answers are out there waiting to be experienced, or, if professionals already have sufficient experience, it assumes they have all of the answers (Hayes, 2014). Therefore, there is no knowledge progression.

Lastly, knowledge generated through experience lacks scalability – just because I have experienced something and believe it to be true does not mean that the 'truth' is shared with others. Truth is contextual, which is why stating something is 'true' is problematic as it might be an individual experience of truth (Biesta, 2014). There is a need to share empirical theories in order to 'test out' which truths are shared. The advancement of knowledge would be further restricted if early years professionals relied too much on experience as the knowledge would be individualised and not distributed for wider validation.

Throughout earlier chapters I have emphasised that professionalism requires the application of knowledge (Furlong, 2000). However, I have also emphasised that knowledges have different structures that can render them more or less meaningful to the knower. Experiential knowledge often feels more relevant to the knower not only because it has been experienced, but also because it will meet the needs of the context. Conversely, theory can feel divorced from the knower as it is knowledge for its own sake, with the knower having no control over the knowledge (see Chapter 3). However, theory has strong structures that support a process of distributing knowledge for challenge and verification, something that experiential knowledge lacks. If experiential knowledge is not distributed, challenged, verified and shared, meanings cannot be reached and the knowledge remains localised. Therefore, there is a need to individually and collectively explore ways in which to challenge and verify experiential knowledge, as well as distribute it for wider scrutiny.

Reflective Practice

Dewey regarded reflection as an important part of experiential learning. Reflection required open-mindedness, responsibility and wholeheartedness. Open-mindedness reflects a willingness to accept other perspectives; responsibility is about a responsible attitude, such as thinking about the needs of children; and wholeheartedness is about being sincere in the process (Hallet, 2013). The reflective process distinguishes between routine action, whereby external forces, habits and authority dominate practice rather than considering the reasons for practice, and reflective action, whereby actions are carefully considered and justified (Craft and Paige-Smith, 2008).

Reflection has become something of an established feature of early years professionalism. Reflection has been positioned as a skill that will enable early years professionals to make sense of the knowledges needed to meet the needs of the context. For example, Kuisma and Sandberg (2008) discuss the role of reflection in the Swedish context for understanding professional practice, Balduzzi (2011) identifies reflection as central to early years professionals within Italy and the role of training in seeking to develop reflection skills (see also Chapter 2), whilst Egan (2009) explores how reflection is utilised in the English context to support those training to understand the interplay between theory and practice. However, despite the commonality in the use of 'reflection' in relation to early years professionalism and its place within initial early years training, this does not mean that there is a consensus on how the skill is performed (Urban et al., 2011).

There are many models of reflective practice, often based on a cyclical approach. For example, readers might be familiar with Kolb's cycle of experience: reflect, conceptualise, experiment, experience; or Gibbs' cycle of description, feeling, evaluation, analysis, conclusion, action plan (Campbell-Barr and Leeson, 2016). As I have explored with my friend and colleague Caroline Leeson, there is a risk that cyclical models can leave a sense of going round and round with little opportunity to jump off the merry-go-round. Thus, whilst Dewey proposed a notion of continuous reflection (Hallet, 2013), this should not be until the point of feeling dizzy.

Most of the models of reflection can be attributed to the work of Dewey and Schön. There is international recognition of the work of Schön in developing the notion of the 'Reflective Practitioner' (Young and Muller, 2014). Schön draws on Dewey to develop the idea that professionals need to be like researchers to develop an 'epistemology of practice' (Furlong, 2000; Young and Muller, 2014). An epistemology of practice is appealing as it is a potentially democratic process for developing a theory of knowledge that is grounded in practice. Within an epistemology of practice, professionals arguably maintain autonomy over the identification of professional knowledge as it comes from within the profession. Within the epistemology of practice, the truth is derived from the actions of professionals. The professional builds up experiences that become the basis of specialised knowledge.

Professional practice does not have a stable context, therefore traditional problem solving does not work, requiring professionals to investigate their practice, including that which cannot easily be described. Schön distinguished between knowing in action, reflection in action and reflection on action. Knowing in action is where thinking is implicit, embedded in the action; reflection in action is when a professional reflects on an incident whilst it is ongoing and the reflection can still be of benefit to the incident; and reflection on action occurs after the incident, when the professional attempts to articulate the incident and to make sense of their actions (Furlong, 2000). There are potential limits to both the 'in' and 'on' action reflection. Reflection in action requires what can be referred to as 'thinking on your feet' being limited to what comes to mind at the point of the incident. Reflection on action occurs after the event, offering more time with which to consider it, but also potentially being limited by the accuracy of the memory of the event (Hayes, 2014). Further, Schön implies that reflection only considers action, but it can also be about policy changes (for example), illustrating that reflection is not solely about experiences in practice. As briefly discussed, the context has different layers that can be the immediate context of professional practice, but also include the context of the early years and the wider cultural context.

Critiques of Schön's model are that it is potentially individualistic, being focused on specifics and not generalisable. There is also a risk of experimentalism, whereby professional knowledge is grounded in professional experiences without consideration of the historical context of knowledge (Young and Muller, 2014). There is an element by which reflective practice reveals a dissatisfaction with propositional knowledge (Furlong, 2000): descriptive, declarative knowledge that is presented as true and justified. The discussion in Chapter 6 on emotionology illustrated that there are knowledges that are 'out there', beyond those of theory, that are important to early years professionals. However, emotionology illustrates how a failure to articulate and distribute the individualistic limits the opportunities for wider scrutiny and validation.

There is a risk that a focus on the individual in conjunction with the experiential de-intellectualises early years professionalism through excluding the historical theoretical hybridity of early years professionalism. Exclusion of the historical context potentially reinforces a division between theory and practice, whereby there is a loss of the longevity and credibility of theory. Further, the strong structure of theoretical knowledge (see Chapter 3) enables it to speak to other knowledges, whereas knowledge that is overly focused on individual, specific reflections cannot speak to other knowledges. A challenge for reflection is that it falls within constructionism and not the scientific approaches of positivism that are favoured in the epistemological hierarchy (see Chapter 3). However, this should not limit the sharing of experiential knowledge and reflection so that it extends beyond the individual.

Professionalism is not individual, as professionals need to meet the needs of the context. Further, professional practice is complex, requiring more than experience alone. The context will include constructions of the purpose of the profession (see Chapter 1), but the purpose of the profession is not constructed through experience (Young and Muller, 2014). Additionally, in accepting that the origins of the profession are morally and ethically orientated (see Chapter 6), professionalism requires the application of knowledge and the execution of moral judgements (Furlong, 2000), but experience will not provide a series of right and wrong moral judgements.

The criticisms of Schön illustrate the need for a model that can bring together theory and practice. It is for this reason that I presented Bernstein's model of Singulars, Regions and Fields of Practice in Chapter 3 (Bernstein, 2000). Bernstein's model provides a framework within which the theoretical and the experiential can come together. The Singulars represent the theoretical knowledge, with their strong structures and sense of history. The Fields of Practice represent the everyday, experiential knowledge, with a recognition that it is the action within the Field of Practice that shapes both practice and professional knowledge. However, there is recognition that the knowledges from one Field may not be transferable to another. Again there is the potential for professional knowledges to be context dependent, so it might be for this reason that Bernstein offers Regions (Young and Muller, 2014).

Within Regions there is both current and future professional knowledge. The current professional knowledge draws upon the theoretical hybridity of the early years knowledge-base, recontextualising disciplines to meet the needs of the Field of Practice. Within Regions, professionals can draw upon knowledges that are common across the profession, the multiple disciplines that shape early years professionalism. However, in facing both theory (Singulars) and practice (Fields of Practice) early years professionalism can draw on both theory and practice in the development of specialised knowledge.

My focus on the work of Bernstein is not a rejection of reflection, but a dual argument that action and professional experience alone will not foster professional knowledge and that there is a need for a more sophisticated analysis of professional practice. There is much to be learnt from professional experience, and reflection provides a starting point with which to articulate professional practice and analyse it. The articulation will support the distribution of knowledge that has been derived from practice, enabling it to be analysed and potentially giving rise to new theories. However, reflection is not just about the action within practice; as already outlined, reflection should encompass opportunities for experimentation (such as 'this might work'), thoughts on policy change, analysis of the role of the profession, concepts of childhood and more (Craft and Paige-Smith, 2008).

Reflection should consider both individual practice and the wider context in order to prevent reflection from being restricted to practice. Considering the wider context includes reflecting on the different layers, such as the immediate context of practice, the early years context and that of wider society. Further, reflection should not solely be an individual exercise, but one that encompasses colleagues in order to foster the open-mindedness that Dewey put forward. Going beyond individual practice and engaging with those outside of the immediate context of professional practice would also enable a consideration of whether the knowledge developed in one Field of Practice is relevant across fields. Therefore, whilst there is much to be gained from reflecting as an individual and with immediate colleagues, there are also opportunities from beyond day-to-day practice.

QUESTION

Who could you reflect with? Develop a network/mind map of the people who are relevant to your professional practice and who could support and contribute to a group reflection.

Why Reflect?

Research from England signals the potential benefits of reflecting on practice. The Effective Provision of Preschool Education (EPPE) project identified that well-qualified, critically reflective staff are seen to run early years settings more effectively and are open to change and challenge (Sylva et al., 2004). In research undertaken with colleagues on what quality early years services might look like for two year olds in England, qualifications and quality were seen as inseparable, with higher qualifications seen to offer early years professionals the opportunity to develop reflective practice skills (Georgeson et al., 2014). There is further work to be done in disentangling the relationship between quality, qualifications and the role, place and development of reflective practice, but the evidence suggests that one attribute of higher qualifications that is important for quality early years services is the development of reflective practice.

The Researching Effective Pedagogy in the Early Years (REPEY) project offers some evidence as to the place of reflective practice for supporting the quality of services and children's subsequent outcomes. The REPEY project identified the importance of sustained shared thinking for fostering social, behavioural and cognitive development in children (Siraj-Blatchford, 2002). The principles of sustained shared thinking are that adults sensitively listen to and observe children and develop conversations accordingly. However, the concept of listening is more than just hearing what it is that children are saying, but encompassing an ethic of care (see Chapter 6) so that that brings forth the other, engrossing in the other, sensitively responding to their needs in relation to the wider context (Wood, 2008). The ethic of care is very practical and demands systematic and critical reflection on human action, but the reflection is not programmable, instead being spaces for opening up and considering alternative perspectives (Dahlberg and Moss, 2005). The process of reflection is therefore far from superficial, requiring engrossment, whilst being conscious of the wider context.

The Foci of Reflection

There is a risk that reflection can become a catch-all term with a series of processes that potentially detract from the reasons to reflect. There is a temptation to reflect on everything and anything, resulting in a negative spiral of critiquing practice and the different layers of the context. Drawing on the work of Bronfenbrenner (1979) and his ecological systems theory, I consider how the different layers of the system can be used as a model with which to consider the different layers of the context and what might be included within them as foci for reflection. Often Bronfenbrenner's ecological model is related to considering children's development, but within early years professionalism it offers the opportunity to consider the complex realities in which early years professionals live their lives and their profession (Dalli et al., 2012).

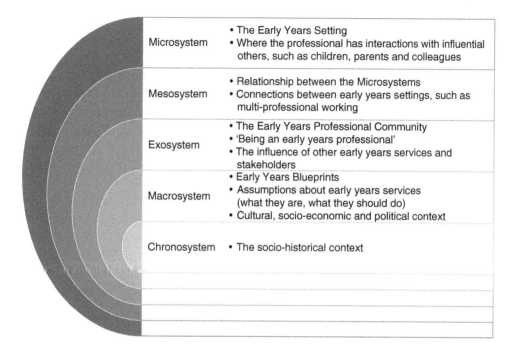

Microsystem	• The Early Years Setting • Where the professional has interactions with influential others, such as children, parents and colleagues
Mesosystem	• Relationship between the Microsystems • Connections between early years settings, such as multi-professional working
Exosystem	• The Early Years Professional Community • 'Being an early years professional' • The influence of other early years services and stakeholders
Macrosystem	• Early Years Blueprints • Assumptions about early years services (what they are, what they should do) • Cultural, socio-economic and political context
Chronosystem	• The socio-historical context

Figure 7.1 The layers of early years professional reflection
Diagram informed by Dalli et al. (2012)

Figure 7.1 is not intended to be an exhaustive list of the possibilities that could be considered within a model of reflection for early years professionalism, but it does provide a framework for detailing the different layers of reflection that I alluded to earlier. Broadly, the Microsystem encompasses the day-to-day practice, experiences and observations of the early years professional as they work with young children. The Exosystem represents the early years community and the commonly held views as to how early years services should operate, such as the predominance of play-based and child-centred practice for early years pedagogy. Between these two layers is the Mesosystem, which represents the interactions between the day-to-day and the commonly held views of the early years community, such as how a child-centred approach is developed in relation to the children in a professional's care. The Macrosystem is then the wider cultural views on early years services and childhood, including the views of policy makers and commonly held assumptions about what is a good childhood. The Chronosystem is the history of early years services, both in regard to how they have developed and how the assumptions about services and childhood have also evolved.

The different layers represent the opportunities for different foci of reflection, such as reflection on day-to-day practice, reflection on the commonly held views of the early years community, reflection on how a professional has been shaped by those commonly held views, the influence of the early years blueprints and the influence of the socio-historical context. Viewing reflection within an ecological model offers the opportunity for a consideration of the individual professional, the early years community, the wider cultural context and the socio-historical context of early years services. Considering the different layers therefore enables an analysis of how an individual's professional practice is shaped by the commonly held views of early years services, the assumptions about what early years services 'do' and how an early years professional 'should' be in relation to the rich history of the multiple theoretical disciplines that have shaped and informed the different layers.

Bronfenbrenner's ecological system enables an appreciation of the different socio-historical contexts present in different countries (Dalli et al., 2012), including accounting for the varying histories of early years services in respective countries. Being country specific limits any potentially universalising characteristic of reflection and its different layers, accounting for the different national, early years and individual contexts that are present. For some, the layers will be contentious (for others harmonious), such as the ways in which the concepts of childhood discussed in Chapter 5 can be variably engaged with. The reference to concepts of childhood provides a reminder that, despite the appreciation for the different contexts, there will be some common constructs that are shared across different cultural contexts.

━━━━━━━━━━ **QUESTION** ━━━━━━━━━━

Using Figure 7.2 as a template, detail what you identify as being important for each layer.

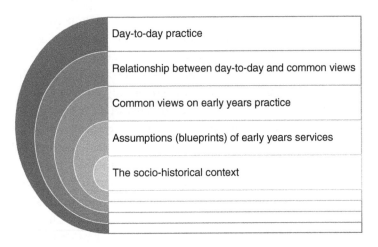

Figure 7.2 Template for reflection

In completing the template readers may find that they have to complete the first and third layers before the second. Readers may also find that as they add to one layer they identify other items to include in other layers. The mapping of the different layers will be anything but neat, as professionals trace the connections between the different layers. The messiness will be symbolic of the Regions discussed in Chapter 3 and the coming together of knowledges for informing professional practice.

Figure 7.2 provides a model with which to begin to explore early years professionalism and what and who is shaping it, but I would also suggest that within the model there is an opportunity to focus on knowledges, including the relationship between knowledges and the power and reach of different knowledges in order to develop more sophisticated solutions to professional practice and to support the advancement of knowledge.

Returning to the work of Bernstein, the Field of Practice can be regarded as being at the centre of Figure 7.2 – the everyday, experiential knowledge that shapes professional practice. The outer rings on Figure 7.2 represent Singulars – the theoretical disciplines that form the multi-disciplinarity of early years professionalism (see Chapters 3 and 4). Regions represent the coming together of the inner and outer rings and the interplay between the individual experiences of professionals and the history of the theoretical disciplines for shaping understandings of the common views of early years practice and assumptions about early years services.

Bernstein did not use Bronfenbrenner's model (or vice versa). My use of Bronfenbrenner is primarily about developing a more visual representation of the coming together of the different knowledges that early years professionals acquire, develop and possess. However, despite this, Bernstein does indicate his interest in exploring the relationship between the different layers.

> The construction of the inner was a guarantee for the construction of the outer. In this we can find the origin of the professions. (Bernstein, 2000: 85)

Not only does the inwardness illustrate a commitment to the profession, it also draws upon the outer in developing the early years knowledge-base. The coming together of the inner and the outer is illustrative of the coming together of the vertical and horizontal discourses (see Chapter 3). However, whilst Figure 7.2 could be reconfigured to consider day-to-day knowledges, the relationship between day-to-day knowledges and common views of the knowledges required for early years services, assumptions of the knowledges within early years professionalism and the socio-historical development of the early years knowledge-base, a focus on knowledges alone will not meet the needs of professional practice.

Throughout the chapters I have emphasised that knowledge alone is not enough, as knowledge needs to be applied within professional contexts. Whilst in this chapter I have cautioned against overly relying on professional practice and experiential knowledge, there is a need to analyse the messiness of Regions in order to reflect on knowledge combinations. In Chapter 4 I explored the distinction between know-that and know-how. Know-that as the expertise, theory and propositions (statements of judgement or hypothesis) cannot transfer directly into knowing how to 'do' early years practice or how to 'be' an early years professional. Instead, professionals need a variety of forms of know-how.

Within Regions (and/or in analysing the different layers), professionals require know-how that is more than just how to apply knowledge. As such, professionals need to know how:

- to combine knowledges
- to evaluate the reliability and validity of the different knowledges
- to negotiate the different knowledges.

The consideration of knowledge combinations is not solely about how theory can inform practice or the opportunity for practice to give rise to new theories, but is about the messiness of professional practice. For me, knowing about knowledge combinations exposes the sensitivities of an ethic of care whereby an early years professional can know about an individual child and their likes and dislikes; know that there are expectations of them, as a professional, to support the child's development; know that there are stated frameworks that outline what is expected of a child at a given age; and know about theories of child development. In the professional's engrossment in the other they are not only bringing forth the needs of the child, but also sensitively combining them with the other layers of knowledges.

In combining knowledges, professionals will evaluate the knowledges and their combinations. Professionals may have preferred theories that help them make sense of their professional practice or hold epistemological assumptions as to what constitutes knowledge resulting in a favouring of neuroscience over socio-cultural theories (for example). However, the evaluation will also be about the ability of the knowledges to meet the needs of the context, such as the usefulness of neuroscience in guiding day-to-day practice. The relationship to the usefulness of practice illustrates the epistemology of practice referred to in relation to Schön, whereby a professional may evaluate the reliability of knowledge based on its ability to facilitate practice in the past.

However, within the evaluation of knowledges, early years professionals will be aware that there are some forms of knowledge that are negotiable and others that are not. Within many national contexts there is an expectation that early years professionals will track, document and demonstrate children's development. The focus on child development may be counter to knowledge of romantic concepts of childhood, but a professional might also know that the focus on development is non-negotiable. Therefore, within the knowledge combinations there may be some artistic licence in how knowledges are combined so that individual epistemological biases can be combined with the expectations of the profession.

Ethical Implications of Reflection

The recognition of the potential for conflict between different knowledges leads to a consideration of the ethical implications of reflection. Firstly, if undertaking reflection with others there needs to be an appreciation that this will involve a process of engaging with how others view the world and this requires respect for the other's perspectives. Secondly, reflection is potentially very exposing, particularly in groups, but also when reflecting as an individual. For example, whilst I have advocated articulating a professional emotionology (see Chapter 6) as part of a wider process of disseminating, testing and building shared understandings of early years professional knowledges, I recognise that the identification of emotions as individual could contribute to a blurring of the personal and the professional self that not everyone will feel comfortable with. Therefore, within any reflection, individual or with others, there is a need to respect what professionals are willing to share.

In respecting what professionals are willing to share, there is also a need to be aware that often reflections will be about others or involve others in some way. Inevitably there is a need to be mindful of the privacy of the self and others in any form of reflection, such as ensuring that others cannot be identified unless they have given consent to do so. However, there is also a need to be mindful of how reflection can potentially lead to moral judgements on or about others. I would therefore suggest that the process of considering the different layers is about identifying any judgements and where they have come from and if they need to be challenged to support a deeper level of reflection than just criticising others.

Conclusion

Within this chapter I have considered how professionals will have an empirical theory of how the world is based upon their experiences, both general ones and those within early years contexts. The learning generated from being a part of a community (both generally and the early years community) is illustrative of socio-cultural theories whereby participation in the community supports a process of coming to know. However, it is not enough to just participate in the community, the participation requires a process of 'doing', testing out knowledges, or testing our hypothesis, whereby the action prevents the knowledge from merely being 'out there'.

The focus on action is central to professionalism and it is, therefore, little wonder that action forms the focus of much reflective practice. Reflection offers the opportunity to support a proactive claiming of professional knowledges in the early years. The focus on professional experiences and practice maintains a focus on the professional and offers the opportunity for new theories to arise from practice. However, there is a risk that the focus on practice becomes individualised, whilst also failing to take into account the long history of theoretical knowledge that is present for early years professionals.

Bernstein's model of Singulars, Regions and Fields of Practice is one where theory and practice can come together within Regions. Within Regions professionals can draw upon both everyday knowledge and the long history of theoretical knowledge. However, reflection is central to the process of considering knowledge combinations, as professionals need to consider how knowledges can be combined and evaluate their usefulness in meeting the needs of practice. Part of the usefulness will also be evaluating the various knowledges, such as that which is seen as reliable and robust knowledge for shaping professional practice.

The use of Bronfenbrenner's ecological model provides a visual tool with which to consider the different knowledges for professional practice. The inner layers represent the everydayness of the Field of Practice, whilst the outer layers represent the long history of the theoretical hybridity of early years professionalism. The model offers an opportunity for both individuals and groups to analyse the knowledges that shape professional practice.

CHAPTER SUMMARY

- Early years professionals have an empirical theory of the world which will be based upon different layers of observations and experiences.
- Professionals learn through being a part of a community, whereby over time participation in the community leads to mastery.
- Relying solely on experience for professional knowledges risks an assumption that people become their most knowledgeable on the day they retire, that knowledge stagnates and has no scalability.
- Reflective practice offers the opportunity to carefully consider and justify actions within practice.
- Reflective practice is commonly referred to within early years professionalism, but there are many different models that can be adopted.
- Reflection requires a consideration of practice in relation to theory, drawing together Singulars and the Field of Practice within Regions.
- Reflection needs to extend beyond the individual and beyond individual Fields of Practice to support the distribution and verification of the knowledges within different fields.

FURTHER READING

Moloney, M. (2018). 'Preparing professionals', *Scéalta Blog | Early Childhood Ireland*. Available at: https://www.earlychildhoodireland.ie/blog/preparing-professionals

In this blog, there is a consideration of the balance between the practical and theoretical training of early years professionals in Ireland. Read the article and consider how you would divide the time between practical and academic (theoretical) training and what would support the integration of the two.

Young, M. and Muller, J. (2014). 'From the sociology of professions to the sociology of professional knowledge', in M. Young and J. Muller (eds), *Knowledge, Expertise and the Professions*. London: Routledge, pp. 3–17.

This is a helpful chapter for considering the distinction between the work of Schön and Bernstein, whilst also offering more detail on Bernstein's model.

8

CONCLUSION

The growing recognition and consideration of early years professionalism has been stimulated by international interest in the social welfare function of early years services and the centrality of the early years workforce for the quality of services. Whilst some countries have an apparent longevity to the professional status of those working in the early years, for others early years has become a new profession. Irrespective of the duration of the professional status of those working in early years services, early years professionals have increasingly become policy objects in many countries. The objectification takes many forms, from requirements to meet particular outcomes (thus shaping pedagogical practice) to dictates on what constitutes the profession through a series of standards and competences to be met. The connection between outcomes and professionalism demonstrates that the knowledges and skills required of a professional will be tied to the role and purpose of the profession. However, whilst policy makers might focus on a professional as a tool to enhance children's development, such a construction of the purpose of the profession might not reflect the views held by parents, children and professionals themselves.

Early years professionals are the meeting point for different perspectives on early years services, children and childhood. Not only will the different perspectives be those belonging to different stakeholders, such as policy makers, parents and children, they will also be the different perspectives that have evolved over time and those that exist between contexts. In Chapter 1, I outlined how a clear challenge for early years professionals is that they find themselves negotiating different stories as to what early years services are and the social purpose that they are seen to fulfil. The different stories contribute to how professionals mediate between different concepts of childhood (for example), often balancing them against each other to inform the ways in which they work with young children (see Chapter 5). Equally (and in conjunction) it might be about balancing expectations in regard to emotionology that exposes how professionals manage the different perspectives on their role (see Chapter 6).

In highlighting that there are many different facets of early years professionalism that an individual is balancing at any one time signals my emphasis on knowledges. Whilst there has been much consideration of the competing pressures on early years professionals, alongside competing perspectives on their role, there has (in my opinion) been less work focusing specifically on what the early years knowledge-base consists of and the knowledges required to support a professional's balancing act. To say that any professional requires more than one knowledge to inform their professional practice is perhaps obvious, but I do believe that early years professionalism is particularly complex in its range of knowledges.

More than Knowing

In Chapter 4, I broadly outlined what constitutes the early years knowledge-base. Key to the discussion was emphasising that early years is multi-disciplinary. Therefore, those who choose to study to become an early years professional will be studying a full range of disciplines, whilst seeking to find a balance between them to inform their professional practice. The informing of professional practice is paramount, as without applying the knowledges in context, an individual cannot be a professional. However, it is not just about how to apply the knowledges, but also about how to combine them, adjusting the weight and measure to meet the needs of the context. Then (if this was not enough) a professional also needs to know how to evaluate the knowledges, both in regard to evaluating knowledge combinations and the rigour of the knowledges. The early years knowledge-base is therefore far more complex than just studying a range of disciplines.

The work of Bernstein, and those who have built upon it (see Chapter 3), has provided a framework for considering the complexity of the different knowledges that exist for informing early years professionalism and their relationship to practice. Whilst the longevity and rigour of theoretical knowledge locate it within vertical discourse, Bernstein's framework provides both the opportunity for professionals to draw on local, everyday knowledge and the potential for new knowledges to be derived from practice. What counts as knowledge has changed over time, and continues to change and evolve. The shift from professionalism being grounded in morals to more technocratic models of professionalism (see Chapter 6) signals a change in what constitutes professional knowledge. Even within the early years knowledge-base there have been shifts in what constitutes knowledge, from the dominance of developmental psychology to the rise of the sociology of childhood (see Chapter 4). Whilst at the time of writing there is consideration of the global knowledge economy, which favours knowledge that can be seen, observed and accounted for, there is little certainty as to the knowledge that will be required for the future.

Predictions of the knowledge needed for the future are not intended as an opportunity for me to write about science fiction or for me to reflect back on how no one could have foreseen that texting and understanding emojis would become essential life skills. Instead, I think that the dissatisfaction with technocratic models of professionalism and the rise in research around the place of emotions in early years professionalism indicate that perspectives on the knowledges required for working with young children are shifting. There remains little certainty as to the knowledges required for the future, but I think there is an evolving appreciation that not all knowledges can be seen and observed.

Shifting perspectives as to what constitutes knowledge, and the specifics as to what kinds of knowledge are needed for early years professionalism, demonstrate that it is not possible to universalise knowledges and skills. Knowledges and skills change with time, not only over centuries, but also over years, months, weeks and even hours – especially within the early years. Coming to know is an ongoing process, whereby the knowing self is always partial and incomplete. Whilst this might create some despondency, the recognition that there is no utopian point of 'knowing' is important as it is this that enables knowledge to keep evolving. Not only do knowledges evolve on a grand scale, on the individual level the continual pursuit of knowledge is what supports professional practice to evolve, develop and improve.

There is a democratic allure within Bernstein's model of professional knowledge as it offers the potential for practice to give rise to new knowledge – for horizontal discourse to become vertical (see Chapter 3). However, I am also aware that my favouring of Bernstein is based upon my own epistemological perspective, and that there are alternatives. For example, I have discussed and recognised the place of post-structural perspectives in challenging biological determinism; questioning the epistemological base of developmental theories and concepts of quality; exploring how dominant discourses seek to discipline human behaviour and the hierarchies of power in the production of knowledge; and, ultimately, opening up the possibility of telling more than one story about early years professionalism. Whilst I think there is much that post-structural perspectives offer, my concern has been that the challenge and questioning within post-structuralism can leave a sense of unknowing – a deconstruction of knowledge until nothing is left. My drawing upon different theoretical perspectives at differing points of my discussion might leave me open to accusations of theoretical cherry picking, but I regard it as establishing existing perspectives on early years professionalism, whilst looking for new ways forward.

My inclusion of Bronfenbrenner in Chapter 7 could be regarded as further evidence of selective theorising, but my choice to adopt Bronfenbrenner's model in regard to reflective practice was not about a full engagement with the ecological model, but a visual representation of the different layers that exist for foci of reflection within early years professionalism. In many respects, the different layers refer back to the different perspectives that I identified earlier and in Chapter 1 that shape early years professionalism. As such, an early years professional needs to consider the full range of perspectives that shape their professional role.

I am aware that in considering the different perspectives and layers of the context that shape early years professionalism, I have not presented an all-encompassing discussion of professional knowledge and skills in the early years. For example, I have only briefly touched upon child protection and multi-professional working, and I am aware that I have not discussed Special Educational Needs. Creating a definitive overview of all of the knowledges and skills required of early years professionals would require a series of volumes as opposed to one book. If I were to consider *all* knowledges, I would need to begin to explore the knowledges required in relation to children's interests, such as football, flowers, the latest TV programmes, dinosaurs, unicorns, etc. When I first started working with children I never appreciated how skilled I would become in making pompoms, illustrating both the unpredictability of knowledge and its expanse. My focus, therefore, has been to consider what might be regarded as the core knowledges and skills for early years professionalism, but I recognise that there will be many other knowledges and skills that readers will also want to consider in relation to their own professionalism.

The Individual and the Social

The consideration of one's own professionalism illustrates that early years professionalism is highly individual, but it is also very social. The individual is well illustrated when considering how the combination of knowledges will vary from professional to professional, accounting for the rich and varied ways in which people approach their professional practice. In particular, emotions are often regarded as highly individual, but as discussed in Chapter 6, they are the product of social interactions. The interplay between the individual and the social has been evident throughout the chapters, such as the individual acquisition of knowledges and skills to ensure employability, alongside the social expectations of the profession. Early years professionals are not situated in vacuums; left to their own devices, their role is very social – dependent on interactions with others – and there is a range of stakeholders who are interested in their professional role, underlined by constructions of the social function of the profession. The early years professional is therefore in a constant negotiation between the social and the individual.

What I find strangely fascinating about early years professionalism is that it is a profession that everyone thinks they can do or they at least assume to know something about it. The assumed knowledges and skills of early years professionalism are likely to be derived from the fact that everyone has had a childhood and many people have daily encounters with children either within their own families or through travelling on public transport or going to the supermarket. However, the assumption that almost anyone can 'be' and 'do' early years professionalism strikes me as strange. Compare early years professionalism to some of the founding professions such as medicine or law – I have been to the doctor's, I have even been in hospital for a night, my mother was a nurse and so I used to spend time helping out at the hospital, but I have never for one moment assumed I could 'be' a doctor and 'do' medicine.

Admittedly, if we trace the history of medicine, there were many people who believed they could do medicine (consider how the red and white stripes of a barber's shop are believed to trace back to when barbers undertook medical procedures). It may be because early years is a new a profession that it results in so many people believing that they can 'do' it and that in the future there will be a greater appreciation of the intricacies of coming to know how to be an early years professional.

My motivation for writing this book has always been to highlight the complexities of coming to know how to work with young children. The complexities of becoming an early years professional are not solely in relation to the range of knowledges that are required or that the knowledges need to be combined to varying extents, applied to meet the needs of the context and evaluated. There is much about early years professionalism that is incredibly knowledgeable and skilled, but I do not yet have the words to fully articulate it. The historical origins of early years services in romanticism and philanthropy will have contributed to the apparent ease of being able to work with children, but as research has advanced and supported a more detailed understanding of early years services and the professionals that work in them, there is a greater appreciation that not everything is *known* about what makes a good early years professional. Just as professional knowledge has no end point, nor does understanding professional knowledge and skills in the early years.

I hope that my exploration of professional knowledge and skills in the early years is the starting point for celebrating the rich and varied ways that people come to know how to work with young children and for recognising the true complexities of the profession. Early years is a highly skilled and extremely knowledgeable profession, encompassing the theoretical and the everyday to meet the needs of the context. Just as I have been shaped by my epistemological position, so too are early years professionals. Early years professionals will be shaped by their individual epistemological perspectives and the stances that they take in combining and applying their knowledges to meet the needs of the context. Early years is thus a highly knowledgeable and skilled profession.

GLOSSARY

COMMUNISM	Generally Communism is a theory of social organisation whereby all property is owned by the community and each person contributes and receives based on a system of their ability and needs.
CULTURAL CAPITAL	The assets that an individual possesses to support their social mobility, such as knowledge, values, language and tastes that symbolically represent the individual's place in society.
EPISTEMOLOGICAL	The theory of knowledge, considering its nature, origin, methods, validity and reach.
FEMINISM	Broadly the advocacy of women's rights and equality of the sexes. Also adopted as philosophical, political and theoretical stances, with varying interpretations.
HETERO-NORMATIVITY	The idea that people fall into distinct and complementary genders with prescribed roles.
PERSONAL ECONOMIC RESPONSIBILITY	Within policy frameworks, personal economic responsibility places an emphasis on individuals to be responsible for their economic viability, rather than relying on the state. For example, individuals should seek employment to lift themselves out of poverty rather than relying on state benefits.
PHILANTHROPIC	A person, persons or organisation that seeks to promote the welfare of others.

POST-STRUCTURAL Often associated with a philosophical movement of the late 20th century that was dissatisfied with the populism of structuralism and a perceived control and monitoring undertaken by state institutions. Post-structuralism offers a way of studying knowledge that rejects the notion of dominant ideals. The studying of an 'object' also requires an analysis of the knowledge that produced the object.

ROMANTICISM Often associated with an arts and literature movement in the late 18th century, the exact period of Romanticism is disputed. The term within early years contexts is used to refer to a philosophical thinking that is frequently attributed to the work of Rousseau and the natural child, pre-disposed to learning.

SOCIAL INVESTMENT Social investment means to invest in people. Often it results in a series of policies that seek to strengthen people's knowledge and skills to support them to participate in employment and other areas of life.

SUPRA-NATIONAL ORGANISATIONS Supra-national organisations are those which transcend geographical, national boundaries. The organisations seek to represent a collective body of ideas to support (and influence) national governments.

REFERENCES

Adams, K. (2008). 'What's in a name? Seeking professional status through degree studies within the Scottish early years context', *European Early Childhood Education Research Journal*, 16(2), 196–209.

Allen, G. (2011). *Early Intervention: The Next Steps*. London: HM Government.

Andrew, Y. (2015). 'What we feel and what we do: emotional capital in early childhood work', *Early Years*, 35(4), 351–65.

Andrew, Y., Corr, L., Lent, C., O'Brien, M., Osgood, J. and Boyd, M. (2016). 'Worthwhile work? Childcare, feminist ethics and cooperative research practices', *Gender and Education*, 30(5): 553–68.

Aslanian, T.K. (2015). 'Getting behind discourses of love, care and maternalism in early childhood education', *Contemporary Issues in Early Childhood*, 16(2), 153–65.

Balduzzi, L. (2011). 'Promoting professional development in Early Childhood Education and Care (ECEC) field: the role of welcoming newcomers teachers', *Procedia – Social and Behavioral Sciences*, 15, 843–9.

Bernstein, B. (1999). 'Vertical and horizontal discourse: an essay', *British Journal of Sociology of Education*, 20(2), 157–73.

Bernstein, B.B. (2000). *Pedagogy, Symbolic Control, and Identity: Theory, Research, Critique* (rev. edn). Oxford: Rowman & Littlefield.

Biesta, G. (2014). 'Pragmatising the curriculum: bringing knowledge back into the curriculum conversation, but via pragmatism', *The Curriculum Journal*, 25(1), 29–49.

Bourdieu, P. (2008). 'The forms of capital', in N.W. Biggart (ed.), *Readings in Economic Sociology*. Hoboken, NJ: Blackwell Publishers, pp. 280–91.

Bowlby, J. (1958). 'The nature of the child's tie to his mother', *The International Journal of Psychoanalysis*, 39, 350–73.

Bowlby, J., Ainworth, M., Boston, M. and Rosenbluth, D. (1956). 'The effects of mother–child separation: a follow-up study', *British Journal of Medical Psychology*, 29(3–4), 211–47.

Brock, A. (2013). 'Building a model of early years professionalism from practitioners' perspectives', *Journal of Early Childhood Research*, 11(1), 27–44.

Brodin, J., Hollerer, L., Renblad, K. and Stancheva-Popkostadinova, V. (2015). 'Preschool teachers' understanding of quality in preschool: a comparative study in three European countries', *Early Child Development and Care*, 185(6), 968–81.

Bronfenbrenner, U. (1979). *The Ecology of Human Development: Experiments by Nature and Design*. Cambridge, MA and London: Harvard University Press.

Cameron, C. (2001). 'Promise or problem? A review of the literature on men working in early childhood services', *Gender, Work and Organization*, 8(4), 430–53.

Cameron, C. (2006). 'Men in the nursery revisited: issues of male workers and professionalism', *Contemporary Issues in Early Childhood*, 7(1), 68–79.

Cameron, C. and Miller, J. (2016). 'The early years professional in England', in M. Vandenbroeck, M. Urban and J. Peeters (eds), *Pathways to Professionalism in Early Childhood Education and Care*. Abingdon: Routledge.

Campbell-Barr, V. (2012). 'Early years education and the value for money folklore', *European Early Childhood Education Research Journal*, 20(3), 423–37.

Campbell-Barr, V. (2014). 'Constructions of early childhood education and care provision: negotiating discourses', *Contemporary Issues in Early Childhood*, 15(1), 5–17.

Campbell-Barr, V. (2015). 'The research, policy and practice triangle in early childhood education and care', in R. Parker-Rees and C. Leeson (eds), *Early Childhood Studies*. Exeter: Learning Matters.

Campbell-Barr, V. (2017a). 'Interpretations of child centred practice in early childhood education and care', *Compare: A Journal of Comparative and International Education*. Epub ahead of print, 1–17.

Campbell-Barr, V. (2017b). 'Quality early childhood education and care – the role of attitudes and dispositions in professional development', *Early Child Development and Care*, 187(1), 45–58.

Campbell-Barr, V. (2018). 'The silencing of the knowledge-base in early childhood education and care professionalism', *International Journal of Early Years Education*, 26(1): 75–89.

Campbell-Barr, V. and Bogatić, K. (2017). 'Global to local perspectives of early childhood education and care', *Early Child Development and Care*, 187(10), 1461–70.

Campbell-Barr, V. and Leeson, C. (2016). *Quality and Leadership in the Early Years*. London: Sage.

Campbell-Barr, V., Georgeson, J. and Nagy Varga, A. (2015). 'Developing professional early childhood educators in England and Hungary: where has all the love gone?', *European Education*, 47(4), 311–30.

Campbell-Barr, V., Georgeson, J., Adams, H. and Short, E. (2018). *Child-centredness in Practice: Report on Output 2*. Plymouth: Plymouth University. Available at: www.plymouth.ac.uk/research/child-centred-diversity-in-quality-early-childhood-education-and-care (accessed 8 August 2018).

Caruso, F. and Sorzio, P. (2015). 'The complex construction of professionalism in ECEC service in Italy', in V. Campbell-Barr and J. Georgeson (eds), *International Perspectives on Early Years Workforce Development*. Northwich: Critical Publishing, pp. 40–54.

Colley, H. (2006). 'Learning to labour with feeling: class, gender and emotion in childcare education and training', *Contemporary Issues in Early Childhood*, 7(1), 15–29.

Commission/EACEA/Eurydice/Eurostat (2014). *Key Data on Early Childhood Education and Care in Europe 2014 Edition*. Luxembourg: Publications Office of the European Union.

Craft, A. and Paige-Smith, A. (2008). 'What does it mean to reflect on our practice?', in A. Paige-Smith and A. Craft (eds), *Developing Reflective Practice in the Early Years*. Maidenhead: Open University Press.

Dahlberg, G. and Moss, P. (2005). *Ethics and Politics in Early Childhood Education*. London: RoutledgeFalmer.

Dalli, C. (2008). 'Pedagogy, knowledge and collaboration: towards a ground-up perspective on professionalism', *European Early Childhood Education Research Journal*, 16(2), 171–85.

Dalli, C., Miller, L. and Urban, M. (2012). 'Early childhood grows up: towards a critical ecology of the profession', in L. Miller, C. Dalli and M. Urban (eds), *Early Childhood Grows up: Towards a Critical Ecology of the Profession*. London: Springer, pp. 3–20.

Di Santo, A., Timmons, K. and Lenis, A. (2017). 'Preservice early childhood educators' pedagogical beliefs', *Journal of Early Childhood Teacher Education*, 38(3), 223–41.

Dillen, A. (2006). 'Children between liberation and care: ethical perspectives on the rights of children and parent–child relationships', *International Journal of Children's Spirituality*, 11(2), 237–50.

Dubovicki, S. and Jukić, R. (2017). 'The importance of acquiring pedagogical and didactic competencies of future teachers – the Croatian context', *Early Child Development and Care*, 187(10), 1557–68.

Duncan, S. and Edwards, R. (1997). 'Lone mothers and paid work: rational economic man or gendered moral rationalities?', *Feminist Economics*, 3(2), 29–61.

Egan, B.A. (2009). 'Learning conversations and listening pedagogy: the relationship in student teachers' developing professional identities', *European Early Childhood Education Research Journal*, 17(1), 43–56.

Elfer, P. (2015). 'Emotional aspects of nursery policy and practice – progress and prospect', *European Early Childhood Education Research Journal*, 23(4), 497–511.

European Commission (2007). *Key Competences for Lifelong Learning: European Reference Framework*. Brussels: European Commission.

European Commission (2014). *Proposal for Key Principles of a Quality Framework for Early Childhood Education and Care: Report of the Working Group on Early Childhood Education and Care under the Auspices of the European Commission*. Brussels: European Commission.

Fenech, M. (2011) 'An analysis of the conceptualisation of "quality" in early childhood education and care empirical research: promoting "blind spots" as foci for future research', *Contemporary Issues in Early Childhood*, (2), 102–17.

Fukkink, R.G. and Lont, A. (2007). 'Does training matter? A meta-analysis and review of caregiver training studies', *Early Childhood Research Quarterly*, 22(3), 294–311.

Furlong, J. (2000). 'Intuition and the crisis in teacher professionalism', in Y. Atkinson and G. Claxton (eds), *The Intuitive Practitioner*. Buckingham: Open University Press.

Furlong, J. and Whitty, G. (2017). 'Knowledge traditions in the study of education', in G. Whitty and J. Furlong (eds), *Knowledge and the Study of Education: An International Exploration*. Oxford: Symposium Books, pp. 13–60.

Gabriel, N. (2017). *The Sociology of Early Childhood: Critical Perspectives*. London: Sage.

Garnier, P. (2011). 'The scholarisation of the French école maternelle: institutional transformations since the 1970s', *European Early Childhood Education Research Journal*, 19(4), 553–63.

Georgeson, J. and Campbell-Barr, V. (2015). 'Attitudes and the early years workforce', *Early Years*, 35(4), 321–32.

Georgeson, J. and Payler, J. (2014). 'Qualifications and quality in the early years foundation stage', in J. Moyles, J. Payler and J. Georgeson (eds), *Early Years Foundations*. Maidenhead: McGraw-Hill Education, pp. 52–64.

Georgeson, J., Campbell-Barr, V., Boag-Munroe, G., Mathers, S., Caruso, F. and Parker-Rees, R. (2014). *Two Year Olds in England: An Exploratory Study*. London: Tactyc. Available at: tactyc.org.uk/wp-content/uploads/2014/.../TACTYC_2_year_olds_Report_2014.pdf (accessed 18 August 2018).

Goldstein, L.S. (1998). 'More than gentle smiles and warm hugs: applying the ethic of care to early childhood education', *Journal of Research in Childhood Education*, *12*(2), 244–61.

Grace, G. (2014). 'Professions, sacred and profane: reflections upon the changing nature of professionalism', in M. Young and J. Muller (eds), *Knowledge, Expertise and the Professions*. Abingdon: Routledge.

Guile, D. (2014). 'Professional knowledge and professional practice as recontextualisation: a social practice perspective', in J. Muller and M. Young (eds), *Knowledge, Expertise and the Professions*. Abingdon: Routledge.

Hakim, C. (2000). *Work-lifestyle Choices in the 21st Century: Preference Theory*. Oxford: Oxford University Press.

Hallet, E. (2013). *The Reflective Early Years Practitioner*. London: Sage.

Hayes, C. (2014). 'The nature of reflective practice', in C. Hayes, J. Daly, M. Duncan, R. Gill and A. Whitehouse (eds), *Developing as a Reflective Early Years Professional: A Thematic Approach*. Northwich: Critical Publishing, pp. 1–21.

Heckman, J. (2000). *Invest in the Very Young*. Chicago: Ounce of Prevention Fund and the University of Chicago Harris School of Public Policy Studies. Available at: www.theounce. org/wp-content/uploads/2017/03/HeckmanInvestInVeryYoung.pdf (accessed 8 August 2018).

Hedges, H. and Cullen, J. (2005). 'Subject knowledge in early childhood curriculum and pedagogy: beliefs and practices', *Contemporary Issues in Early Childhood*, *6*(1), 66–79.

Held, V. (2002). 'Care and the extension of markets', *Hypatia*, *17*(2), 19–33.

Hendrick, H. (1997). 'Constructions and reconstructions of British childhood: an interpretative survey, 1800 to the present', in A. James and A. Prout (eds), *Constructing and Reconstructing Childhood: Contemporary Issues in the Sociological Study of Childhood*. London: Routledge, pp. 34–62.

Hochschild, A.R. (2003). *The Managed Heart: Commercialization of Human Feeling*. Berkeley: University of California Press.

Holmes, J. (2012). *John Bowlby and Attachment Theory*. Hoboken, NJ: Taylor & Francis.

Hordern, J. (2016). 'Knowledge, practice, and the shaping of early childhood professionalism', *European Early Childhood Education Research Journal*, *24*(4), 508–20.

Hordern, J. (2017). 'Bernstein's sociology of knowledge and education(al) studies', in J. Furlong and G. Whitty (eds), *Knowledge and the Study of Education: An International Exploration*. Oxford: Symposium Books.

Jenks, C. (2004). 'Constructing childhood sociologically', in M. Kehily (ed.), *Introduction to Childhood Studies*. Maidenhead: McGraw-Hill Education.

Jensen, A.S., Broström, S. and Hansen, O.H. (2010). 'Critical perspectives on Danish early childhood education and care: between the technical and the political', *Early Years*, *30*(3), 243–54.

Jensen, J.J. (2015). 'Placement supervision of pedagogue students in Denmark: the role of university colleges and early childhood centres', *Early Years*, *35*(2), 154–67.

Johnson, D. (2000). *Intuition, Culture and the Development of Academic Literacy*. Buckingham: Open University Press.

Jones, C.E. (2015). '"… For the love of children and the joy of childhood": the reported values, beliefs and practices of male practitioners within early childhood education and care in England', *Journal of Early Childhood Research*, *14*(4), 407–30.

Jones, P. (2014). 'Training and workforce issues in the early years', in G. Pugh and B. Duffy (eds), *Contemporary Issues in the Early Years*. London: Sage, pp. 255–72.

Karlsson, L.M. (2015). 'Bridging "the gap" – linking workplace-based and university-based learning in preschool teacher education in Sweden', *Early Years*, 35(2), 168–83.

Kehily, M.J. (2010). 'Childhood in crisis? Tracing the contours of "crisis" and its impact upon contemporary parenting practices', *Media, Culture and Society*, 32(2), 171–85.

Kinkead-Clark, Z. (2017). 'Early childhood care and education in Jamaica: stakeholders' perceptions of global influences on a local space', *Early Child Development and Care*, 197(10), 1484–95.

Krieg, S. (2010). 'The professional knowledge that counts in Australian contemporary early childhood teacher education', *Contemporary Issues in Early Childhood*, 11(2), 144–55.

Kuisma, M. and Sandberg, A. (2008). 'Preschool teachers' and student preschool teachers' thoughts about professionalism in Sweden', *European Early Childhood Education Research Journal*, 16(2), 186–95.

Lave, J. and Wenger, E. (1991). *Situated Learning: Legitimate Peripheral Participation*. Cambridge: Cambridge University Press.

Lazzari, A. (2012). 'Reconceptualising professionalism in early childhood education: insights from a study carried out in Bologna', *Early Years*, 32(3), 252–65.

Li, H. and Chen, J.J. (2016) 'Evolution of the early childhood curriculum in China: the impact of social and cultural factors on revolution and innovation', *Early Child Development and Care*, 187(1), 1471–83.

Lipponen, L.T., Hilppö, J.A. and Rajala, A.J. (2018). *Cultures of Compassion*. London: British Educational Research Association. Available at: www.bera.ac.uk/blog/cultures-of-compassion-in-early-childhood-education (accessed 8 August 2018).

Loreman, T. (2011). *Love as Pedagogy*. Rotterdam: Sense Publishers.

Lundkvist, M., Nyby, J., Autto, J. and Nygård, M. (2017). 'From universalism to selectivity? The background, discourses and ideas of recent early childhood education and care reforms in Finland', *Early Child Development and Care*, 187(1), 1543–56.

MacFarlane, K. and Lewis, P. (2012). 'United we stand: seeking cohesive action in early childhood education and care', *Contemporary Issues in Early Childhood*, 13(1), 63–73.

MacNaughton, G. (1997). 'Feminist praxis and the gaze in the early childhood curriculum', *Gender and Education*, 9(3), 317–26.

MacNaughton, G. (2005). *Doing Foucault in Early Childhood Studies: Applying Poststructural Ideas*. Abingdon: Routledge.

Maier-Höfer, C. (2015). 'Attitude and passion: becoming a teacher in early childhood education and care', *Early Years*, 35(4), 366–80.

Marshall, J. (2014). *Introduction to Comparative and International Education*. London: Sage.

McGillivray, G. (2008). 'Nannies, nursery nurses and early years professionals: constructions of professional identity in the early years workforce in England', *European Early Childhood Education Research Journal*, 16(2), 242–54.

McNess, E., Arthur, L. and Crossley, M. (2015). ' "Ethnographic dazzle" and the construction of the "Other": revisiting dimensions of insider and outsider research for international and comparative education', *Compare: A Journal of Comparative and International Education*, 45(2), 295–316.

Miller, L. (2008). 'Developing professionalism within a regulatory framework in England: challenges and possibilities', *European Early Childhood Education Research Journal*, 16(2), 255–68.

Miller, L. and Cameron, C. (2014). 'International perspectives: themes and issues', in L. Miller and C. Cameron (eds), *International Perspectives in the Early Years*. London: Sage, pp. 1–10.

Moloney, M. (2010a). 'Professional identity in early childhood care and education: perspectives of pre-school and infant teachers', *Irish Educational Studies*, 29(2), 167–87.

Moloney, M. (2010b). 'Unreasonable expectations: the dilemma for pedagogues in delivering policy objectives', *European Early Childhood Education Research Journal*, 18(2), 181–98.

Moss, P. (2006). 'Structures, understandings and discourses: possibilities for re-envisioning the early childhood worker', *Contemporary Issues in Early Childhood*, 7(1), 30–41.

Moss, P. (2014a). 'Early childhood policy in England 1997–2013: anatomy of a missed opportunity', *International Journal of Early Years Education*, 22(4), 346–58.

Moss, P. (2014b). *Transformative Change and Real Utopias in Early Childhood Education: A Story of Democracy, Experimentation and Potentiality*. Abingdon: Routledge.

Moss, P. (2017). 'Power and resistance in early childhood education: from dominant discourse to democratic experimentalism', *Journal of Pedagogy*, 8(1), 11–32.

Moss, P., Dahlberg, G., Grieshaber, S., Mantovani, S., May, H., Pence, A., Rayna, S., Swadener, B.B. and Vandenbroeck, M. (2016). 'The Organisation for Economic Co-operation and Development's international early learning study: opening for debate and contestation', *Contemporary Issues in Early Childhood*, 17(3), 343–51.

Nagy Varga, A., Molnar, B., Palfi, S. and Szerpi, S. (2015). 'Hungarian perspectives on the early years workforce development', in V. Campbell-Barr and J. Georgeson (eds), *International Perspectives on Early Years Workforce Development*. Northwich: Critical Publishing, pp. 105–17.

Noddings, N. (2010). 'Moral education in an age of globalization', *Educational Philosophy and Theory*, 42(4), 390–6.

Noddings, N. (2012). 'The caring relation in teaching', *Oxford Review of Education*, 38(6), 771–81.

Nutbrown, C. and Clough, P. (2014). *Early Childhood Education: History, Philosophy and Experience* (2nd edn). London: Sage.

Nygård, M. and Krüger, N. (2012). 'Poverty, families and the investment state', *European Societies*, 12(5), 755–77.

Oberhuemer, P. (2005). 'Conceptualising the early childhood pedagogue: policy approaches and issues of professionalism', *European Early Childhood Education Research Journal*, 13(1), 5–16.

Oberhuemer, P. (2014). 'Seeing early childhood issues through a European lens', in L. Miller and C. Cameron (eds), *International Perspectives in the Early Years*. London: Sage, pp. 13–31.

Oberhuemer, P., Schreyer, I. and Neuman, M. (2010). *Professionals in Early Childhood Education and Care Systems: European Profiles and Perspectives*. Opladen: Barbara Budrich Publishers.

OECD (2011). *Starting Strong III: A Quality Toolbox for Early Childhood Education and Care*. Paris: OECD.

OECD (2014). *PISA 2012 Results: What Students Know and Can Do* (Volume I, Revised edition, February 2014). Paris: OECD.

OECD(2015a). *'Call for Tenders: International Early Learning Study (100001420)'*. Paris: OECD.

OECD (2015b). *Starting Strong IV: Monitoring Quality in Early Childhood Education and Care*. Paris: OECD.

Onnismaa, E.-L., Tahkokallio, L. and Kalliala, M. (2015). 'From university to working life: an analysis of field-based studies in early childhood teacher education and recently graduated kindergarten teachers' transition to work', *Early Years*, 35(2), 197–210.

Osgood, J. (2006). 'Professionalism and performativity: the feminist challenge facing early years practitioners', *Early Years: An International Journal of Research and Development*, 26(2), 187–99.

Osgood, J. (2009). 'Childcare workforce reform in England and "the early years professional": a critical discourse analysis', *Journal of Education Policy*, 24(6), 733–51.

Osgood, J. (2012). *Narratives from the Nursery: Negotiating Professional Identities in Early Childhood*. Abingdon: Routledge.

Osgood, J. and Robinson, K.H. (2017). 'Celebrating pioneering and contemporary feminist approaches to studying gender in early childhood', in K. Smith, K. Alexander and S. Campbell (eds), *Feminism(s) in Early Childhood: Using Feminist Theories in Research and Practice*. Singapore: Springer Singapore, pp. 35–47.

Page, J. (2018). 'Characterising the principles of professional love in early childhood care and education', *International Journal of Early Years Education*, 26(2), 125–41.

Page, J. and Elfer, P. (2013). 'The emotional complexity of attachment interactions in nursery', *European Early Childhood Education Research Journal*, 21(4), 553–67.

Parker-Rees, R. (2015). 'Concepts of childhood: meeting with difference', in R. Parker-Rees and C. Leeson (eds), *Early Childhood Studies: An Introduction to the Study of Children's Lives and Children's Worlds* (4th edn). London: Sage, Online Editions.

Payler, J.K. and Locke, R. (2013). 'Disrupting communities of practice? How "reluctant" practitioners view early years workforce reform in England', *European Early Childhood Education Research Journal*, 21(1), 125–37.

Penn, H. (2011). *Quality in Early Childhood Services*. Maidenhead: McGraw-Hill.

Penn, H. (2012a). 'Childcare markets: do they work?', in E. Lloyd and H. Penn (eds), *Childcare Markets: Can They Deliver an Equitable Service?* Bristol: Policy Press, pp. 19–13.

Penn, H. (2012b). 'Shaping the future: how human capital arguments about investment in early childhood are being (mis)used in poor countries', in N. Yelland (ed.), *Contemporary Perspective on Early Childhood Education*. Maidenhead: Open University Press, pp. 49–65.

Piper, C. (2008). *Investing in Children: Policy, Law and Practice in Context*. Cullompton: Willan Publishing.

Pisani, L., Dyenka, K., Sharma, P., Chhetri, N., Dang, S., Gayleg, K. and Wangdi, C. (2017). 'Bhutan's national ECCD impact evaluation: local, national, and global perspectives', *Early Child Development and Care*, 187, 1511–27.

Pound, L. (2011). *Influencing Early Childhood Education: Key Figures, Philosophies and Ideas*. Maidenhead: McGraw-Hill/Open University Press.

Powell, S. (2010). 'Hide and seek: values in early childhood education and care', *British Journal of Educational Studies*, 58(2), 213–29.

Press, F. (2015). 'The Australian early childhood education and care workforce: feminism, feminisation and fragmentation', in V. Campbell-Barr and J. Georgeson (eds), *International Perspectives of Early Years Workforce Development*. Northwich: Critical Publishing, pp. 65–77.

Public, K., Panayiotou, S., McGinigal, S., Kent, K., Smit, C., Witsø, C. and Edwards-Hughes, E. (2017). *Survey of Childcare and Early Years Providers England 2016: SFR: 09/2017*. London: Department for Education. Available at: www.gov.uk/government/statistics/childcare-and-early-years-providers-survey-2016 (accessed 8 August 2018).

Rajala, A.J. and Lipponen, L.T. (2018). 'Early childhood education and care in Finland: compassion in narrations of early childhood education student teachers', in S. Garvis, S. Phillipson and H. Harju-Luukkainen (eds), *International Perspectives on Early Childhood Education and Care: Early Childhood Education in the 21st Century Vol I*. Abingdon: Routledge, pp. 64–75.

Randall, V. (2000). *The Politics of Child Daycare in Britain*. Oxford: Oxford University Press.

Rekalidou, G. and Panitsides, E.A. (2015). 'What does it take to be a "successful teacher"? Universities' role in preparing the future early-years workforce', *Early Years*, 35(4), 333–50.

Rhedding-Jones, J. (2005). 'Decentering Anglo-American curricular power in early childhood education: learning, culture, and "child development" in higher education coursework', *Journal of Curriculum Theorizing*, 21(3), 143–65.

Rosen, D.M. (2007). 'Child soldiers, international humanitarian law, and the globalization of childhood', *American Anthropologist*, 109(2), 296–306.

Selbie, P. and Clough, P. (2005). 'Talking early childhood education', *Journal of Early Childhood Research*, 3(2), 115–26.

Simpson, D. (2010). 'Being professional? Conceptualising early years professionalism in England', *European Early Childhood Education Research Journal*, 18(1), 5–14.

Siraj-Blatchford, I. (2002). *Researching Effective Pedagogy in the Early Years*. London: DfES (Department for Education and Skills).

Skeggs, B. (1997). *Formations of Class and Gender: Becoming Respectable*. London: Sage.

Stearns, P.N. and Stearns, C.Z. (1985). 'Emotionology: clarifying the history of emotions and emotional standards', *The American Historical Review*, 90(4), 813–36.

Strohmer, J. and Mischo, C. (2016). 'Does early childhood teacher education foster professional competencies? Professional competencies of beginners and graduates in different education tracks in Germany', *Early Child Development and Care*, 186(1), 42–60.

Sylva, K., Melhuish, E., Sammons, P., Siraj-Blatchford, I. and Taggart, B. (2004). *The Effective Provision of Pre-school Education (EPPE) Project: Final Report: A Longitudinal Study Funded by the DfES 1997–2004*. London: Institute of Education, University of London/Department for Education and Skills/Sure Start.

Taggart, G. (2016). 'Compassionate pedagogy: the ethics of care in early childhood professionalism', *European Early Childhood Education Research Journal*, 24(2), 173–85.

Thomson, R., Kehily, M.J., Hadfield, L. and Sharpe, S. (2011). *Making Modern Mothers*. Bristol: Policy Press.

Tobin, J. (2005). 'Quality in early childhood education: an anthropologist's perspective', *Early Education and Development*, 16(4), 421–34.

United Nations (2015). 'Sustainable Development Goals – United Nations'. Available at: https://sustainabledevelopment.un.org/ (accessed 8 August 2018).

Uprichard, E. (2008). 'Children as "being and becomings": children, childhood and temporality', *Children and Society*, 22(4), 303–13.

Urban, M. (2008). 'Dealing with uncertainty: challenges and possibilities for the early childhood profession', *European Early Childhood Education Research Journal*, 16(2), 135–52.

Urban, M., Vandenbroek, M., Lazzari, A., Peeters, J. and Van Laere, K. (2011). *Competence Requirements in Early Childhood Education and Care (CoRe)*. London and Ghent: University of East London, University of Ghent and European Commission Directorate-General for Education and Culture.

Urban, M., Vandenbroeck, M., Van Laere, K., Lazzari, A. and Peeters, J. (2012). 'Towards competent systems in early childhood education and care: implications for policy and practice', *European Journal of Education*, 47(4), 508–26.

Van Laere, K., Peeters, J. and Vandenbroeck, M. (2012). 'The education and care divide: the role of the early childhood workforce in 15 European countries', *European Journal of Education*, 47(4), 527–41.

Van Laere, K., Van Houtte, M. and Vandenbroeck, M. (2018). 'Would it really matter? The democratic and caring deficit in "parental involvement"', *European Early Childhood Education Research Journal*, 26(2), 187–200.

Vandenbroeck, M. and Peeters, J. (2008). 'Gender and professionalism: a critical analysis of overt and covert curricula', *Early Child Development and Care*, 178(7–8), 703–15.

Vandenbroeck, M., Peeters, J. and Bouverne-De Bie, M. (2013). 'Lifelong learning and the counter/professionalisation of childcare: a case study of local hybridizations of global European discourses', *European Early Childhood Education Research Journal*, 21(1), 109–24.

Veraksa, N. and Sheridan, S. (2018). *Vygotsky's Theory in Early Childhood Education and Research: Russian and Western Values*. Abingdon: Routledge.

Vincent, C. and Braun, A. (2011). '"I think a lot of it is common sense …": early years students, professionalism and the development of a "vocational habitus"', *Journal of Education Policy*, 26(6), 771–85.

Visković, I. and Višnjić Jevtić, A. (2017). 'Development of professional teacher competences for cooperation with parents', *Early Child Development and Care*, 187(10), 1569–82.

Walkerdine, V. (1984). 'Developmental psychology and the child-centred pedagogy: the insertion of Piaget into early education', in J. Henriques, W. Hollway, C. Urwin, C. Venn and V. Walkerdine (eds), *Changing the Subject: Psychology, Social Regulation and Subjectivity*. Abingdon: Routledge, pp. 152–202.

Ward, U. (2018). 'How do early childhood practitioners define professionalism in their interactions with parents?', *European Early Childhood Education Research Journal*, 26(2), 274–84.

Wastell, D. and White, S. (2012) 'Blinded by neuroscience: social policy, the family and the infant brain', *Families, Relationships and Societies*, 1(3), 397–414.

West, A. and Noden, P. (2016). *Public Funding of Early Years Education in England: An Historical Perspective*. London: London School of Economics and Political Science, Department of Social Policy and the Nuffield Foundation. Available at www.nuffieldfoundation. org/sites/default/files/files/Nuffield%20Final%20Report%20historical%2027%20 September%202016.pdf (accessed 8 August 2018).

Wickett, K. (2017). 'Exploring the transition to school: are we all talking the same language?', in S. Dockett, R. Perry and W. Greisel (eds), *Families and the Transition to School*. London: Springer.

Willan, J. (2017). *Early Childhood Studies: A Multidisciplinary Approach*. Basingstoke: Palgrave Macmillan.

Winch, C. (2004). *Philosophy and Educational Policy: A Critical Introduction*. London: RoutledgeFalmer.

Winch, C. (2010). *Dimensions of Expertise: A Conceptual Exploration of Vocational Knowledge*. London: Bloomsbury.

Winch, C. (2014). 'Know-how and knowledge in the professional curriculum', in M. Young and J. Muller (eds), *Knowledge, Expertise and the Professions*. Abingdon: Routledge, pp. 47–60.

Wood, E. (2008). 'Listening to young children: multiple voices, meanings and understandings', in A. Paige-Smith and A. Craft (eds), *Developing Reflective Practice in the Early Years*. Maidenhead: Open University Press, pp. 108–21.

Young, M. (2007). *Bringing Knowledge Back in: From Social Constructivism to Social Realism in the Sociology of Education by Young*. Abingdon: Routledge.

Young, M. and Muller, J. (2007). 'Truth and truthfulness in the sociology of educational knowledge', *Theory and Research in Education*, 5(2), 173–201.

Young, M. and Muller, J. (2014). 'From the sociology of professions to the sociology of professional knowledge', in M. Young and J. Muller (eds), *Knowledge, Expertise and the Professions*. Abingdon: Routledge, pp. 3–17.

INDEX